# A PADDLER'S GUIDE
## TO ONTARIO'S COTTAGE COUNTRY

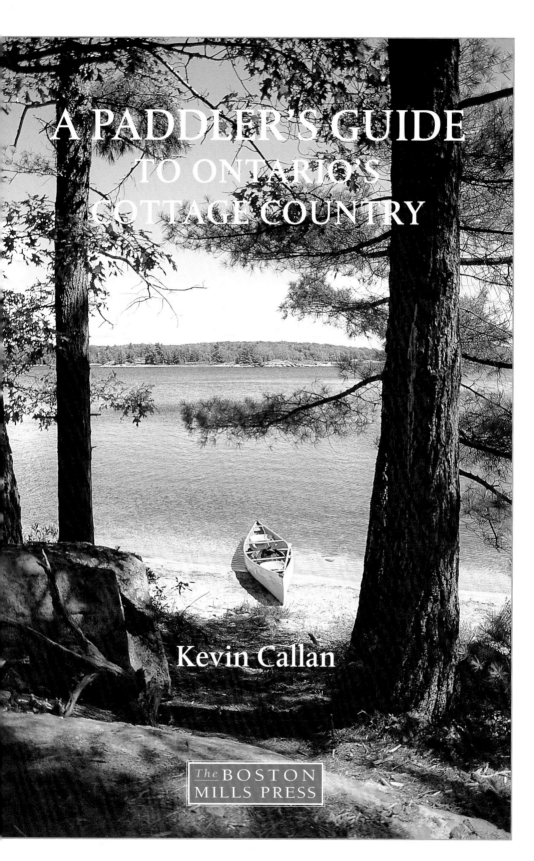

# A PADDLER'S GUIDE
## TO ONTARIO'S
## COTTAGE COUNTRY

### Kevin Callan

*The* BOSTON
MILLS PRESS

A BOSTON MILLS PRESS BOOK

Published by Boston Mills Press, 2003
Copyright © 1993, 2003 by Kevin Callan

First printing this edition, 2003

**National Library of Canada Cataloguing in Publication**

Callan, Kevin
    A paddler's guide to Ontario's cottage country / Kevin
Callan.

Previously published under title: Cottage country
canoe routes.

Includes bibliographical references.
ISBN 1-55046-383-7

1. Canoes and canoeing—Ontario—Guidebooks. 2.
Ontario—Guidebooks. I. Title.

GV776.15.O5C34 2003    797.1'22'09713    C2002-904576-2

Publisher Cataloging-in-Publication Data (U.S.) is available.

Published in 2003 by
BOSTON MILLS PRESS
132 Main Street
Erin, Ontario N0B 1T0
Tel 519-833-2407
Fax 519-833-2195
e-mail books@bostonmillspress.com
www.bostonmillspress.com

IN CANADA:
Distributed by Firefly Books Ltd.
3680 Victoria Park Avenue
Toronto, Ontario M2H 3K1

IN THE UNITED STATES:
Distributed by Firefly Books (U.S.) Inc.
P.O. Box 1338, Ellicott Station
Buffalo, New York 14205

Cover design by Gillian Stead
Interior design and map drawings by Mary Firth
Photographs by Kevin Callan
Printed and bound in Canada by Friesens, Altona,
    Manitoba

The publisher acknowledges the financial support
of the Government of Canada through the Book
Publishing Industry Development Program for its
publishing efforts.

## ACKNOWLEDGMENTS

As with all book projects, it would be impossible to complete my research
without the help of so many people. First, I would like to sincerely thank all
my canoe companions who agreed to tag along with me: Scott Roberts, Peter
Fraser, Mike Walker, Doug Galloway, Brian Reid, Mark van Stempvoort, Noel
Hudson, my dog, Bailey, and especially my wife, Alana.

Thanks to editor Kathy Fraser and designer Mary Firth for their out-
standing talents. I would also like to thank the staff of the Parry Sound,
Bancroft and Minden Districts of the Ministry of Natural Resources for their
assistance throughout my research; Wildrock Outfitters for all their help
and, especially, enthusiasm; and last, but certainly not least, Jim Stevens at
Eureka, Bill at Ostrom Packs and Glenn Fallace from Voyageur Canoes for
supplying me with some great gear on this and other writing projects.

# Contents

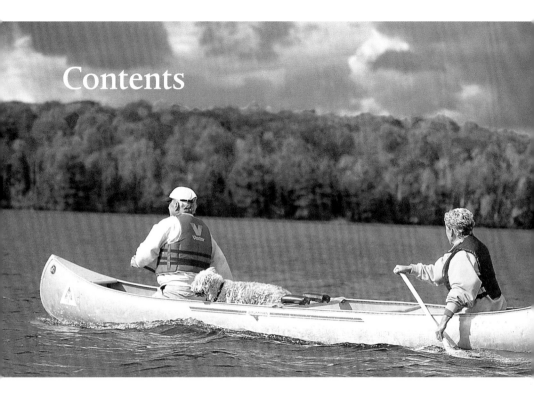

# Preface

**I CAN'T QUITE SEEM TO HELP MYSELF COME SPRING.** The moment the lakes and rivers open up, my paddle hand begins to itch and I find myself once again blindly quitting my job so that I can spend the entire summer season in a canoe. At the end of the season I generally find myself rich in spirit but poor at the bank.

One spring season several years back, break-up came unusually early, and after a long winter of watching Bill Mason films and rereading Sigurd F. Olson's canoe essays, I was more than ready to leave reality and head for the northern waterways. However, after my first trip, I found myself being called back from the wild by my debts. That summer I forced myself to give up the pursuit of being a full-time canoeist, moved to the city and got a job.

I worked for a company situated on the main street, above a stuffy bar, where most of the staff spent their lunch hours. I had it all: a desk, push-button phone and pale blue cubicle next to another pale blue cubicle. The only window in the whole office was in front of the coffee machine. I left my desk so often to get a coffee that my workmates began to tease me about having a caffeine addiction. I just wanted to look out the window.

By midsummer it was obvious I had to find some way to escape, at least for the weekends. Then, one Friday afternoon, I overheard one of the secretaries talking to the boss about canoeing at the cottage the weekend before. My ears perked up when I heard the word canoe, and I jumped into the conversation, asking, "Where can you canoe in cottage country?"

By day's end, the secretary had drawn me a map of a two-day canoe route accessible from the lake her cottage was on. She told me the route was maintained by the Ontario Ministry of Natural Resources, with campsites and portages marked, and it was all free of charge! The next morning, after a three-hour drive from the city, I found myself canoeing through the semi-wilderness of cottage country.

And it was the series of cottage country canoe routes compiled in this guidebook that saved my sanity. For the next two years, I continued to work the nine-to-five grind, escaping each weekend to paddle one of these more than 20 canoe routes through the wilds of Georgian Bay, Muskoka, the Haliburton Highlands and the Kawarthas.

The routes, which I discovered by browsing through old guidebooks and government pamphlets published before the 1970s, were perfect. Each one took no longer than two days to complete, and, except for a couple of routes that had

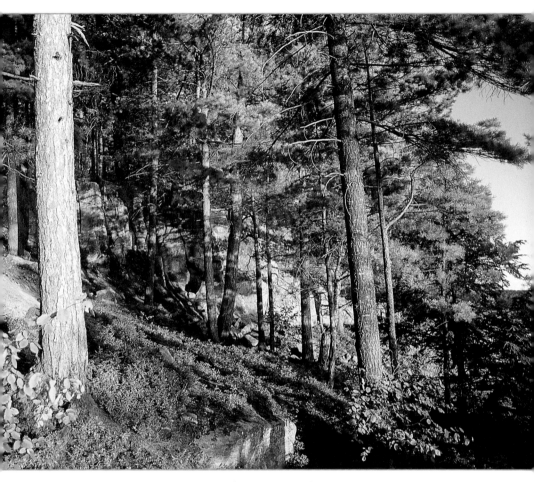

*Shoelace Lake, one of the author's favorite trout-fishing destinations each spring.*

been developed in active provincial or federal parks, no reservations had to be made and no fee was required. The campsites were first come, first served. To guarantee a spot, I just headed out late Friday night or early Saturday morning. It was basically hassle-free.

The routes themselves have changed somewhat since then. Some of them are being overused by canoeists and at the same time are receiving little or no maintenance by the government. Some have actually become provincial parks and now have stricter regulations. But they all still have that huge advantage of providing a quick and easy getaway — whether you have a desk job in the city or are in hot pursuit of obtaining a full-time career in canoeing.

# Georgian Bay
## The Sixth Great Lake

**ETIENNE BRÛLÉ, CHAMPLAIN'S PRIME SCOUT,** arrived on Georgian Bay in 1610, by way of the French River while in search of a route to the Orient. One can imagine this young explorer, not even 18 years of age, looking out over the Great Lake, yearning to paddle across the expanse of water and become the first to discover the southern sea. Instead, he remained with the Huron who were camped along the rugged northeastern shoreline, and when Champlain arrived five years later, he acted as interpreter.

By the time he was 30, Brûlé cared more for the intense life in the bush than God and king. This led Champlain to accuse him of being a traitor. He concluded, "Whatever happens you will always have a worm gnawing at your conscience." Shortly after this incident, Brûlé was — depending on the accounts you read — either killed during a brawl over a Native woman and subsequently eaten by tribe members, or murdered for political reasons, possibly because of his dealings with the Seneca or another tribe feared by the Huron.

When the Europeans "discovered" the sixth Great Lake, they named it Georgian Bay, in honor of King George IV. Soon, canots du maître, symbols of success, cluttered the freshwater travelway. Made of birchbark, these magnificent canoes were powered by beasts of burden — the voyageurs.

By the mid-19th century, the Huron were scattered and their culture greatly diminished as their former homeland soon saw small but bustling European settlements. With the European settlements came the exploitation of natural resources. By 1874 there were seven logging mills in the Georgian Bay area, and by 1890 the forests that once carpeted the shoreline were being rafted away to the States. The Bay was booming.

Yet today, along the lands that were once inhabited by the legendary Huron, there still exist islands sprinkled with juniper and pine, and inland waters with the same wilderness appeal that made Brûlé eventually betray his king and country.

# Beausoleil Island

**LEGEND HAS IT THAT KITCHITEWANA,** the great giant, was the architect of all the islands of Georgian Bay. With his monstrous hands, Kitchitewana scooped huge chunks of earth and rock from the mainland and threw them across the sky. Dozens of inlets were carved into the mainland by the giant's fingers, and the handfuls of rock and earth eventually fell into Georgian Bay to form the 30,000 Islands. When Kitchitewana was finished his work, he became sleepy and took two steps away from Beausoleil Island, to the island that is now called Giant's Tomb, and then stretched out to rest. Some people believe, however, that the Giant's Tomb is not a final resting place for Kitchitewana. It is said that one day the giant will awaken and fill the entire bay with earth and rock, and on this day the world will end.

Let's assume that Kitchitewana will remain in a peaceful slumber as you paddle toward Beausoleil Island, one of the 29 islands that constitute Georgian Bay Islands National Park. The park makes an excellent off-season weekend canoe trip during early spring or late fall, when the water is free of heavy boat traffic.

The 17-mile-long (28 km) island is located directly across from Honey Harbour (take Muskoka Road 5, off Highway 400/69, west to Honey Harbour). Parking and a launching site are available at Honey Harbour Marina, just north of town. From here you can plan one of three outings. Your first option is to paddle northwest, up the Main Channel, between Little Beausoleil Island and Deer Island, and make camp on either Godettes, Cherry or at Honeymoon Bay. Your second option is to paddle the Main Channel, then bear left through Little Dog Channel to use the Blueberry, Chimney or Sandpiper sites. Or you may choose simply to travel west, straight through Big Dog Channel, and make camp on Tonch Point. All destinations are designated sites equipped with firepits, stone stoves, firewood, picnic tables and vault toilets. During the busy season, be sure to phone ahead (705-756-5909) to make reservations.

Campsites on Tonch Point and Chimney Bay are well protected from the wind, as they are located on the eastern shore. I much prefer to camp along the more rugged, windswept northern sections of the island. All of the sites are close to a number of unique hiking trails. Dossyonishing Trail and Fairy Lake Trail are my two favorite hikes.

While hiking on Beausoleil Island keep an eye out for Ontario's endangered eastern Massasauga rattlesnake. The park is one of the few homes left for this almost extinct snake. Approximately 70 to 200 rattlers live on the island, but chances are you'll never see one. If you do come across a Massasauga along the

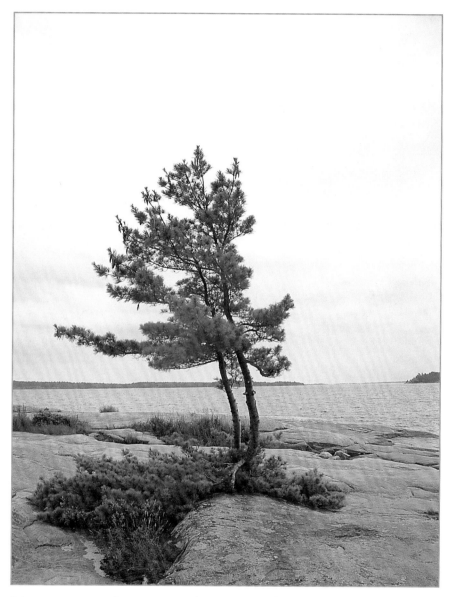

*Most canoeists prefer to camp on the more rugged, windswept northern section of Beausoleil Island.*

trail or in camp, simply leave it alone. You literally have to step on this timid creature before it will strike. My left foot came inches from a Massasauga while hiking across the island's northern tip, and the snake simply sounded its rattle, something like a muffled cicada, and we both slithered away in opposite directions. More dangerous than the Massasauga rattlesnake and considerably more common is the island's infestation of poison ivy. Make sure that you know how to identify this three-leaved plant before heading out on the trail.

In December of 1929 the Department of the Interior announced the birth of a new park: "The Dominion Government has secured twenty-nine islands in Georgian Bay, which are to be set aside for national park purpose. These islands...are of rare beauty and varying sizes...and it will be a consoling thought to the public to know that they are to have retained for their use some portion of Northern Ontario's earthly paradise."

Since the first warden's cabin was constructed in 1931, Beausoleil Island has been a major tourist attraction. The park has gone through a number of changes since its birth, not only to fulfill the needs of thousands of visitors, but out of a need to protect the island from these people.

A weekend on Beausoleil Island today makes more sense than it did in the past. This is not because of the physical changes in the park, for the land has been just as scarred by settlement as other semi-wilderness areas; it is due rather to changes in the philosophy of Georgian Bay Islands National Park management. The park's recreational events have changed from dog derbies to educational and entertaining nature interpretation programs. Rattlesnakes and poison ivy patches are protected, and shoreline wetlands are no longer fogged with pesticides. The park has become a vehicle for preservation and certainly a fine destination for canoeists.

## BEAUSOLEIL ISLAND

**TIME** 1–2 days

**DIFFICULTY** This is considered a novice route, but it should be noted that rough water out on Georgian Bay and heavy boat traffic, especially along the Main Channel, can be extremely hazardous at times.

**PORTAGES** No portages exist for this route.

**FEE** A fee is required for overnight access (a Parks Canada self-registration system is in effect) and making a reservation is highly recommended.

**ALTERNATIVE ACCESS** None

**ALTERNATIVE ROUTE** None

**FISH SPECIES** Both bass and pike fishing can be good at times.

**KAYAK FRIENDLY** This route is actually more suitable for kayakers than canoeists.

**OUTFITTERS**
SWIFT CANOE & KAYAK
(GEORGIAN BAY)
Highway 400 North

Box 604
Waubaushene, Ontario
L0K 2C0
1-800-661-1429
georgianbay@swiftcanoe.com

WHITE SQUALL WILDERNESS SHOP
R.R. 1
Nobel, Ontario
P0G 1G0
705-342-5324
or
19 James Street
Parry Sound, Ontario
P2A 1T4
705-746-4936
www.whitesquall.com

**FOR MORE INFORMATION**
PARKS CANADA
Georgian Bay Islands National Park
Box 28
Honey Harbour, Ontario
Canada
P0E 1E0
705-756-2415
reservations: 705-756-5909
e-mail: infogbi@pch.gc.ca

**TOPOGRAPHIC MAP** 31 D/13

# McCrae Lake

**THE GIBSON–MCDONALD ROUTE** is one of my favorite Georgian Bay spring getaways. The Gibson River's ragged rapids, the Bay's scenic splendor, and the historic treasures of the inland lakes all beckon to me. But over the years I've altered my routine trip down the Gibson to the Bay and then up through McCrae and McDonald Lakes. Now I simply canoe into McCrae via McDonald and, while tenting on the lake, take a couple of leisurely days to poke about.

To reach the access point, take Georgian Bay Road west of Highway 400, originally Highway 69, approximately 30 miles (50 km) south of Parry Sound. The parking lot and portage to MacDonald Lake is located directly off the ramp that exits from the 400. During long weekends or summer holidays, the parking lot and portage can be cluttered with canoes and canoeists, so choose the date of your trip accordingly.

From McDonald's southern inlet, paddle north until you come to a beaver dam on your left. A quick liftover might be necessary at the dam, depending on whether the beaver is busier building up the stick pile than the canoeists are tearing the obstacle down.

Once over the dam, paddle directly across the small bay to the next portage. The 275-yard (250 m) path works its way around a small falls flowing into McCrae. Watch your footing: the steep, rocky incline can be quite treacherous. As well, take note that a snowmobile club has recently constructed a bridge over the cascade, which has become a bit of a hazard, not to mention an eyesore.

A narrow, weedy channel takes you out into the open waters of McCrae. By keeping to your right, you will eventually reach the main body of the lake. As you enter the lake, the rock outcrops to your left and the main island's large northern tip provide excellent tent sites, but I prefer to make the extra pilgrimage down the southern end of the lake and set up camp below a sheer granite ridge.

After pitching your tent, take the afternoon to travel out on the Bay and visit the two historic sites of the former Muskoka Mills. Paddle up through the western channel of McCrae, taking the 11-yard (10 m) portage into the waters of Georgian Bay. Just after the portage, you will see a shrine along the rocky ledge to your left. The story goes that a man staying at a cabin on McCrae accidentally injured himself during a hunting expedition. His wife, who was ailing from whooping cough at the time, managed to drag him to their boat. She then successfully navigated the channel you just portaged over — which was at the time a very dangerous stretch of rapids — and got her husband to Midland by way of

*Waiting in line to use the portage into McCrae Lake.*

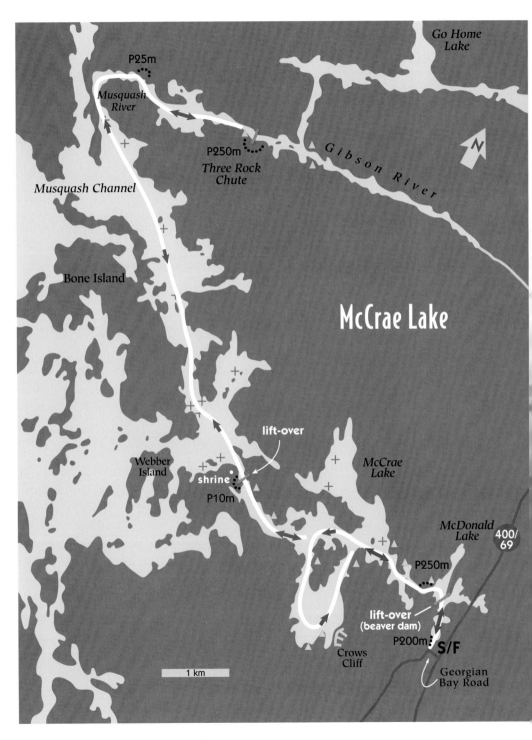

Georgian Bay. At Midland he received medical treatment that saved his life. Because he was glad to have survived and relieved that the whole ordeal was over, the man built the shrine to thank God (and, I gather, his wife).

After you have had a chance to admire the private sanctum, head straight out from the portage, between the main shore and Bone Island. The large island is part of Georgian Bay Islands National Park. Keep following the Georgian Bay shoreline to the mouth of the Musquash River.

At the bend in the river, you will see submerged logs and iron rungs, the only visible remnants of the area's logging heyday. Here, in 1871, the region's largest water-powered sawmill produced 8,500,000 feet of lumber from 80,000 pine logs during a six-month season. The town, Muskoka Mills, had a population of 400, with over 80 employees working for the mill. The lumber was shipped to Owen Sound, Collingwood and Chicago. In 1895, however, the standing timber was exhausted, and the ring of the axe and screech of the saw soon grew silent. Muskoka Mills quickly became a ghost town.

If you paddle up the Musquash River to Three Rock Chute, you can view the birthplace of lumber manufacturing in the Muskoka watershed. Either pole or make the 27-yard (25 m) portage on the left to avoid a small set of rapids. Then paddle across the wide section of the river and go up through a narrow, rocky channel to the base of the falls.

In the early 1850s an entrepreneur by the name of William Hamilton first noticed the huge pines growing along the lower branches of the Musquash River. Three years later he decided to exploit the area and built a small water-powered sawmill on the island at Three Rock Chute. However, the mill only operated for a few years before giving way to the vastly larger Muskoka Mills.

Another perfect outing to make while camped on McCrae Lake is a hike along a well-developed trail that follows the shoreline of McCrae's lower section. The path, developed by the Toronto-based Five Winds Touring Club, is marked by yellow markers and the odd rock cairn. The trail actually starts off from the parking lot at the access point, meanders along the southern shoreline of McCrae, then heads north across the 11-yard (10 m) portage between McCrae and Georgian Bay toward the Gibson River. I found the path by accident the last time I camped on McCrae. While searching for firewood behind my campsite, I came across a series of yellow markers and followed them westward. Approximately 40 minutes later, I discovered a small pond, home to over half a dozen great blue herons. After taking a peek at the heron rookery and photographing the elaborate stick nests built high up in dead trees, I quickly tiptoed away from the nursery. If you come across the rookery, make sure to do the same, as even minor disturbances can cause wary parents to abandon their nests, or young to leave before they can fly and survive on their own.

If canoeing up the Musquash or hiking toward the Bay doesn't appeal to you, then unpack your rod and reel, and fish the weedy bays and rocky shoals for pike. I've caught a few monsters in McCrae in my time.

To return to your vehicle, paddle back via the same route you took into McCrae Lake. Before going, however, make sure to double-check your campsite for the forgotten tent peg, ball of shiny tinfoil or the inconspicuous twist-tie. In other words, leave the place the way you would like to find it.

## MCCRAE LAKE

**TIME** 1–2 days

**DIFFICULTY** A perfect novice trip.

**PORTAGES** 2 (both of which must be doubled back on).

**LONGEST PORTAGE** 275 yards (250 m)

**FEE** McCrae Lake is on Crown land and is part of a proposed Living Legacy Provincial Park. No fee is required for Canadian citizens.

**ALTERNATIVE ACCESS** Six Mile Lake Provincial Park, east of Highway 400/69.

**ALTERNATIVE ROUTE** You can make it a full loop by using Six Mile Lake and the Gibson River.

**FISH SPECIES** Walleye can be caught in the Musquash/Gibson River, especially in spring and fall, and bass and pike are found throughout the route.

**KAYAK FRIENDLY** The portages en route are relatively short, making use of a kayak possible.

**OUTFITTERS**
SWIFT CANOE & KAYAK
(GEORGIAN BAY)
Highway 400 North
Box 604
Waubaushene, Ont
L0K 2C0
1-800-661-1429
georgianbay@swiftcanoe.com

WHITE SQUALL WILDERNESS SHOP
R.R. 1
Nobel, Ontario
P0G 1G0
705-342-5324
or
19 James Street
Parry Sound, Ontario
P2A 1T4
705-746-4936
www.whitesquall.com

**FOR MORE INFORMATION**
MINISTRY OF NATURAL RESOURCES
Parry Sound District Office
7 Bay Street
Parry Sound, Ontario
P2A 1S4
705-746-4201

**TOPOGRAPHIC MAP** 31 D/13

*Above: McCrae Lake is usually free of crowds during the off-season.*
*Below: Alana takes it easy while we float down Georgian Bay's Moon River.*

# Moon River

**SINCE THE MOON RIVER** is only two hours from Metro Toronto, I figured it couldn't possibly compare to some of the more northern trips I've done. But still, while driving north on Muskoka's Highway 69, I would always slow down while passing over the Moon River bridge, take a peek over the guardrail, and wonder what it would be like to spend a weekend paddling down to Georgian Bay.

Then, last spring, I did just that — only to discover that I was right. It wasn't at all like the rivers in the Far North. Second-growth forests crowded the banks, a maze of cottages had been built out on the Bay, and hordes of boaters gathered at the river's mouth to swim, fish and generally trash the place. Obviously, it wasn't virgin wilderness. To me, however, it still presented a sense of what was once wild. For canoeists looking for a simple two-day jaunt to recharge their batteries, I think an adventure on the Moon River is sometimes all that's really needed.

The starting point for the Moon River is on the north side of the Highway 69 bridge and to the left of the roadway. Before heading out, however, arrange to have a second vehicle shuttled to the take-out at the Moon River Marina. To get there, drive north on Highway 69 for 4.5 miles (7 km) and turn left onto Muskoka Road 11. Then, after the town of Mactier (almost 4 miles [6 km] in from the highway), take the Healey and Kapikog Lake Road until you pass the entry point for Massasauga Provincial Park (a distance of about 10.5 miles [17 km]), and then another 1.25 miles [2 km] to the marina, where you must pay a moderate fee for parking in their lot before heading back to the river.

Almost immediately past the put-in is a long stretch of rapids called the Seven Sisters. The first rapid comes with no obvious portage, except for a rugged trail on the right, and it must be run or lined down. The second and third, however, are both small chutes, and must be portaged along the rocks to the right. The remaining four are just shallow, rock-strewn rapids, not too severe but all of them exciting, as long as the water levels stay up. If levels are low, you'll have to wade or line down most of them.

Next, after a 2-mile (3 km) calm stretch, is Curtain Chute. This is place where the bodies of two drowned canoeists — Jack Kim and Bong Sung Lee — were recovered during the spring of 1997. Their deaths attest to the severity of the rapids and the importance of the 240-yard (220 m) portage that runs along the top of the rock ledge to the left. The accident occurred during a spring outing at, surprisingly, 2:30 A.M. According to police reports, one of the seats in their

10-year-old, 14-foot canoe gave way and caused it to tip over. Considering the temperature of the water was down to about 40°F (5°C), and neither of the two men was wearing a lifejacket, they didn't stand much of a chance.

Downstream from Curtain Chute, after the river narrows and then bulges, spreading out around a flattened island carpeted in swamp maple, Twin Rapids comes into view. Here, the river is divided into two main channels by a large island of rock and pine. You will first spot the right channel, a rock-studded chute with a 200-yard (180 m) portage on the right and prime campsites on either side of the drop. The left channel is just around the corner. It has a much more vertical drop to it, making an extremely steep and hazardous put-in for the 130-yard (120 m) portage on the right, which also happens to be covered in poison ivy.

Both channels can be taken. Note, however, that both end with a set of rapids. The left has a small chute that can easily be portaged 55 yards (50 m) on the left or, in low water, can be simply lifted over on the right. The right channel is a different story, though. It has a much sharper drop with no direct way to walk around it except for a rugged bush trail on the left.

The Moon River converges at the end of the two channels. Around the corner to the left is Moon Falls. The cascade drops twice before flushing out into the waters of Georgian Bay. You can either take on the full 490-yard (450 m) portage on the right or shorten your walk by paddling the elongated pool in between.

Possible campsites are all around this spot. However, even though the tumbling cascade makes for a dramatic place to spend the night, I strongly recommend you set up camp upriver, either above or below Twin Rapids. Here you won't be bothered by the crowds of cottagers gathering for a day's outing. As well, the network of rock ledges, tumbled boulders, and fallen cedars hanging low over the bank make for excellent bass-fishing an hour before dusk.

From Moon Falls it's a simple case of navigating through the maze of rocky islands scattered throughout Arnolds Bay, Moon River Bay and, finally, Woods Bay. And as long as you keep close to the right-hand shoreline, especially after passing Isle of Delight, you'll find it easy to locate the docks of Moon River Marina. Be warned, however, that you'll have to make an early-morning paddle here — not only to avoid the brisk winds that quickly make paddling unbearable, but also to get off the water before the local Sea-doo population begins to swarm around you.

Woods Bay

Blackstone Harbour

Moon River Marina **F**

Access to Massasauga Provincial Park

Isle of Delight

Woods Bay Marina

**Alternative Finish**

Moon River Bay

**Moon River**

1 km

Arnolds Bay

Healey & Kapikog Lake Road

PR450m

**Moon Falls**

PL70m

PL150m

PR120m

**Twin Rapids**

PR180m

MACTIER

11

69

Route is continued from top of facing page.

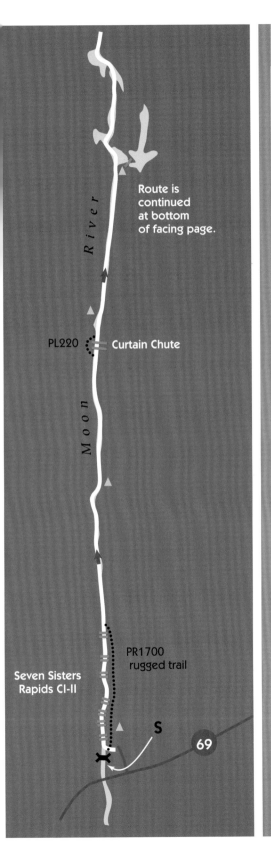

Route is continued at bottom of facing page.

*River*

PL220 ⋯ — Curtain Chute

*Moon*

PR1700
rugged trail

Seven Sisters
Rapids CI-II

S

69

# MOON RIVER

**TIME** 2 days

**PORTAGES** 6

**LONGEST PORTAGE**
490 yards (450 m)

**DIFFICULTY** The Moon's Seven
Sister Rapids are dangerous
during high water, but after early
spring the river calms down and
is perfect for the novice.

**FISH SPECIES** Bass and pike can
be caught along the entire river
and walleye can be caught below
Moon Falls.

**KAYAK FRIENDLY** No, unless
you choose to head directly to
Moon Falls from the marina
access.

**FEE** The route travels through
Crown land, where no fee is
required for Canadian citizens.
However, a fee is charged to park
your vehicle at the Moon Marina.

**ALTERNATIVE ROUTE** None

**OUTFITTERS**
WHITE SQUALL WILDERNESS SHOP
R.R. 1
Nobel, Ontario
P0G 1G0
705-342-5324

**FOR MORE INFORMATION**
MINISTRY OF NATURAL RESOURCES
Parry Sound District Office
7 Bay Street
Parry Sound, Ontario
P2A 1S4
705-746-4201

**TOPOGRAPHIC MAP** 31 E/4

## MASSASAUGA WILDLANDS

I've spent countless weekends paddling through the south section of Georgian Bay, traveling from island to island out in the Bay and then portaging inland to explore the dozens of crystal-clear lakes. With all my visits combined, however, I'm not even close to covering the sum of this vast pocket of isolated wilderness that the locals refer to as the Massasauga Wildlands.

From a protection and heritage-appreciation point of view, the value of this area, which comprises 11,976 hectares (29,590 acres), is second only to Algonquin Provincial Park. It should come as no surprise then that Ontario Parks has declared it a provincial park, officially Massasauga Provincial Park. An endless number of canoe trips can be taken through this park. My own personal favorite routes are the Clear Lake Loop and Spider Bay, both perfect two-day jaunts.

# Clear Lake Loop

**THE CLEAR LAKE LOOP STARTS OFF** at the Ontario Parks access point on Three Legged Lake. To reach the government dock, turn left off Highway 400 (originally Highway 69) on James Bay Junction Road, just south of Oastler Provincial Park. Then take your first left onto Bluechalk Road. Eventually you'll come to Three Legged Lake Road on the right. Follow the dirt road until you reach the Ontario Parks parking lot located on the left-hand side of the road. I usually drive down the steep hill to the government dock first, unload my pack and canoe, then drive back to the parking lot to park my vehicle. Make sure not to leave your car down by the dock or you will have an angry cottager to deal with on your return.

From the dock, head straight out across Three Legged Lake toward the big island. Then paddle along the island's right side, where there's less speedboat traffic. The first portage (350 yards [318 m]) into Spider Lake is well used by both canoeists and local fishermen, who store their small aluminum boats at the end of the portage.

Spider Lake is appropriately named. Its countless bays form an entangled watercourse in which one can easily become lost. Canoeists should carry a set of detailed topographical maps and a compass to help find their way along the interwoven arms of this large inland lake. A few good campsites can be found on Spider Lake, if you arrive at the access point shortly before sundown on a Friday evening.

From the portage into Spider Lake, paddle directly across what appears to be more of an isolated pond than part of the lake, and on to a short, shallow

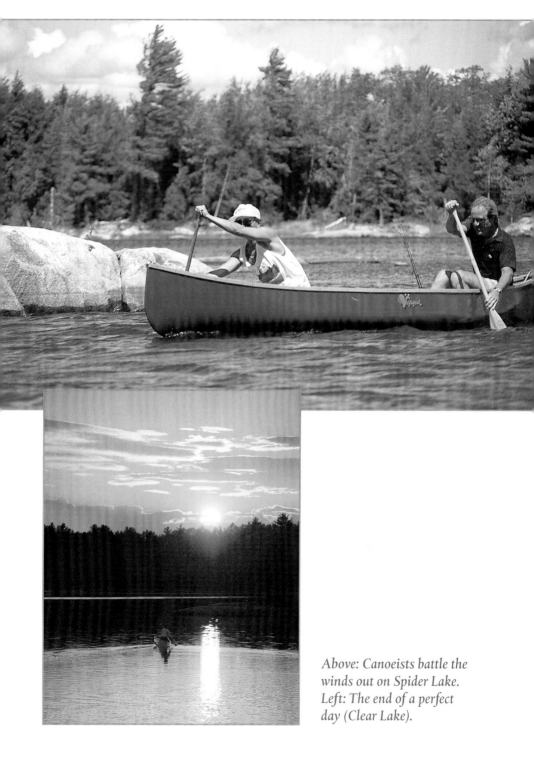

*Above: Canoeists battle the
winds out on Spider Lake.
Left: The end of a perfect
day (Clear Lake).*

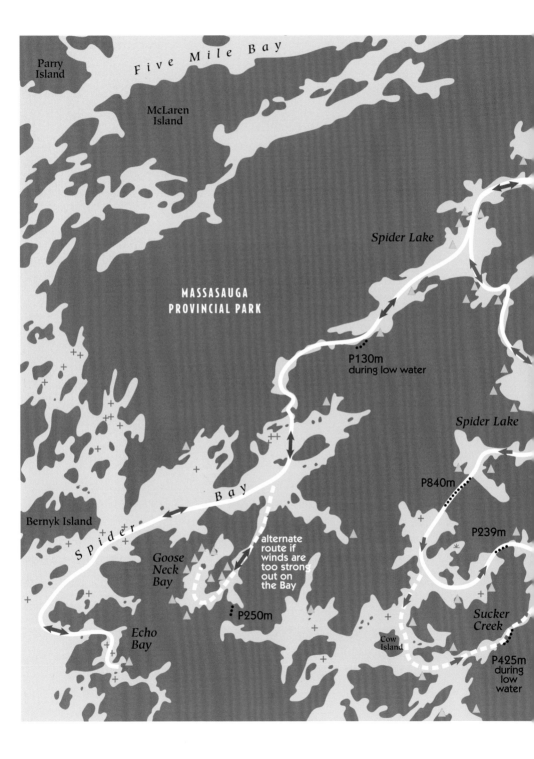

Parry
Island

McLaren
Island

Five Mile Bay

Spider Lake

MASSASAUGA
PROVINCIAL PARK

P130m
during low water

Spider Lake

P840m

P239m

Bay

Bernyk Island

Spider

Goose
Neck
Bay

alternate
route if
winds are
too strong
out on
the Bay

P250m

Cow
Island

Sucker
Creek

Echo
Bay

P425m
during
low
water

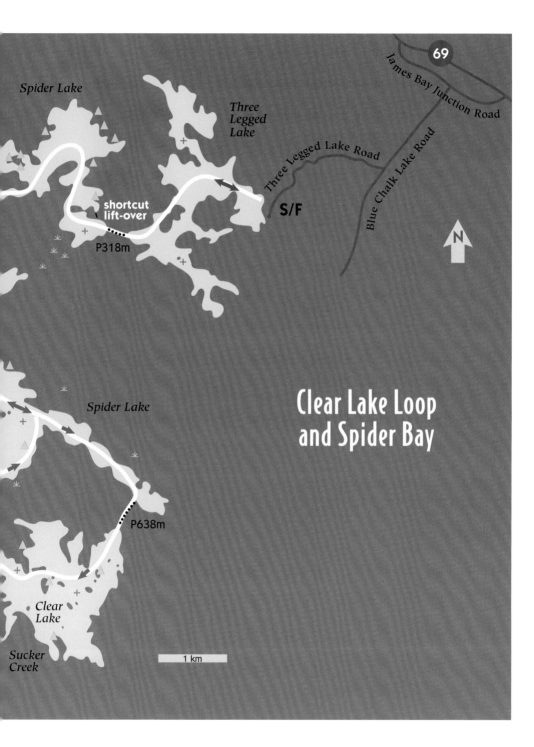

**69**

James Bay Junction Road

Spider Lake

Three
Legged
Lake

Three Legged Lake Road

Blue Chalk Lake Road

shortcut
lift-over

**S/F**

P318m

N

Spider Lake

# Clear Lake Loop
## and Spider Bay

P638m

Clear
Lake

Sucker
Creek

1 km

channel to the right. Head north until the lake opens up, then stay close to the left shoreline, where a long channel takes you to Spider Lake's southwestern inlet. Spider Lake opens up again before you follow the narrow inlet south toward the Clear Lake portage. Here the first hint of Georgian Bay arrives in the wind, a cool breeze redolent of salty seaweed. Gulls and terns play in the winds, piercing the air with their raucous cries, and an expanse of open water with flecks of white-capped waves provides an oceanlike vista.

At this point you will become aware of this route's only disadvantage: You never actually see Georgian Bay. As a result, you feel slightly cheated when you turn tail again toward inland waters.

As you make your way south, you will see that rock outcrops, crowned with stunted oak and pine, line the shores of Spider Lake. This rugged landscape typifies the geology of the Parry Sound Greenstone Belt. The Greenstone Belt consists of a variety of geological formations, including dikes and lava flows. Gouges, chatter marks and ground moraines from the most recent glacial period can also be seen.

If you are lucky, the wind will be at your back while you head down this long southern inlet. With a makeshift sail fashioned from spare paddles and a tent fly, I've navigated my canoe down this stretch of water toward the Clear Lake portage in half an hour or less.

The portage is marked and located on the right shore, where the bay narrows. Take note, however: Just before the marked portage another worn-down path goes into the bush. Make sure you are on the right trail. If you suddenly discover that the portage disappears into an alder swamp, you have taken the wrong path. Believe me, I speak from experience.

The portage into Clear Lake is a lengthy one, totaling 700 yards (638 m), but Clear Lake's scenic splendor makes the journey well worthwhile. This isolated lake, blessed with almost half a dozen island campsites, is one of the finest week-end resorts a canoeist could ever wish for. My favorite site is on one of the large islands in the center of Clear Lake. The island is shaped like a J, with the perfect tent space located in the J's inner loop. A patch of pines protects you from the wind, but a bald outcrop of rock juts out in the open so you can catch a breeze to keep the bugs at bay. The island even has a natural sandy beach that receives the early morning sun.

There are three ways to return to the access point the next day. You can either take the familiar 700-yard (638 m) portage back to Spider Lake, paddle to the southwestern bay of Clear Lake (using the 465-yard [425 m] portage marked to the left of a garden of water lilies and swamp ooze and leading directly to the Bay) or carry over the 260-yard (239 m) portage located almost directly west of my favorite island.

If you return via the same portage you came in on, you miss the chance of christening your canoe on the waters of Georgian Bay. If you choose the second route and water levels are low, then the trip before and after the 465-yard (425 m) portage located to the southwest can end up being a grueling mudbath. The portage directly west is well maintained by the local fishermen and is probably your best choice.

Farther out into the Bay lies Crooked Island, which was home to the first fire outpost, between 1913 and 1936. The forest rangers working out of the fire camp were the first to link the inland lakes with a network of portages. Traveling via canoes equipped with a pump and hand tools, the rangers patroled the entire area throughout fire season. Eventually new and cheaper fire control methods shut down the ranger station, leaving a converted cottage to mark the historic island site.

After finishing the 260-yard (239 m) portage, stay close to the shoreline to your right so as to locate the trail leading from a large isolated bay back to Spider Lake. The portage is 920 yards (840 m) in length and can be found just to the left of the remains of an old homestead. The first time I used this portage, the trail marker was missing and I had to scour the shoreline for a good half-hour before locating the path leading to Spider Bay. This was not a pleasant experience, as I got caught in a heavy thunderstorm.

Once you have looped back over to Spider Lake and paddled northeast up a narrow inlet, you will come to a T-intersection. Head to the left and you will quickly recognize the lake once again and be able to return via Spider Lake to the Three-Legged Lake access point.

# Spider Bay

**THE SPIDER BAY ROUTE** is for the more experienced canoeist. Georgian Bay, a freshwater sea, can quickly sculpture waves to the height of hills, and these waves will roll with an unbridled violence against your canoe.

The route uses the same access point as the Clear Lake Loop. Take the Three-Legged Lake portage into Spider Lake, and as the waters of Spider head out into Georgian Bay, just keep going. Directly west, at the end of Spider Lake, a 142-yard (130 m) portage leads you from the inland lake to the eastern tip of Spider Bay. The portage was once home to a log slide that lumber companies employed to flush logs down to the Bay, where they were shipped out on three-masted schooners.

At the end of the portage, make your way through the shallow channel lined with thick aquatic greenery and mud-caked islands decorated with blue irises and red cardinal flowers. Farther out on Spider Bay, the waters open up, giving you a view of a distant skyline hovering over the waters of Georgian Bay.

The rocky islands and peninsulas of Spider Bay are covered with elaborate cottages. As you paddle by, terns play in the wind above you and cormorants sitting on top of the mounds of rocks eventually take off, leaving the islands covered in seabird dung. If you're like me, the majestic mood of Georgian Bay, with its flat blue horizon, will draw you forward like a magnet.

Once you navigate through Spider Bay, head out toward the expanse of open water, broken only by stark islands and steel-hulled tankers. Camp out along Spider Bay's north shore or search for a protected inlet to the south.

For the history buff, the north shore is a playground. Scattered remnants of a short-lived mining era around the turn of the century mark the graves of five known mine sites located to the north.

A few years ago, a friend and I paddled out to Spider Bay for the weekend. Unfortunately, constant downpour and heavy winds forced us to alter our plans to explore the isolated islands carpeted with ripe blueberry bushes. Like a couple of drenched dogs with tails between our legs, we paddled to the safety of Goose Neck Bay. Rains on Georgian Bay, especially during hot August days, always develop into magnificent thunderstorms. Gigantic clouds, frighteningly black, blow in with a vengeance. Brian (my canoe companion that weekend) and I sat in our canoe, hunched over, depressed by the change of weather. The raindrops struck the lake so hard that small columns of water erupted inches into the air. As a result, we had no choice but to beach our vessel on a rocky island covered in wet juniper bushes.

There we were, huddled under an outstretched tarp, eating soggy sandwiches and soup, feeling betrayed by the weather predictions that the announcer had given on the car radio before we headed out.

During the night, as I curled up in fetal position in my sleeping bag, I listened through the rage of the storm for the echoing blasts of ships' horns as they made their way up the arm of Lake Huron. Every time a ship bellowed its haunting sound, I would try to imagine the fear each sailor must have felt while attempting to navigate through such a storm before wooden hulls were replaced with steel.

One of the most talked about shipwrecks in the area was the *Waubuno*. Built in 1865, the vessel was the lifeline between Parry Sound and the outside world. On Friday, November 21, 1879, the ship was preparing to leave the port in Collingwood for its final northward journey of the season. A northwest gale ravaging Georgian Bay convinced Captain J. Burkett to stay in port until the storm subsided. Once the passengers heard of the delay, some opted to spend the night at a local hotel. But about 4 A.M., thinking the storm had eased enough for safe passage, the captain blew the whistle and headed into Georgian Bay, leaving

*Preparing to wait out an approaching storm in one of Georgian Bay's protective inlets.*

behind those passengers in the hotel. They were the lucky ones. The 10 passengers, 14 crewmen and the captain traveled north toward Parry Sound. Past Christian Island the storm raged harder, forcing the *Waubuno* to weather it out around the islands south of Copperhead Island.

Only the ghosts of the wreck can tell what really occurred after the captain dropped anchor near Haystack Rocks. Historians speculate what happened next. According to Ron Terpstra's *Historical Report: Blackstone Harbour Massasauga Wildlands Provincial Park*, "The anchors held briefly, but the ship was battered by the rough seas, so bad that the upper works began to break, and the anchors tore loose from the anchor chains. The ship 'slid' downwind, and at Black Rock (near the Haystacks), she was picked up by the breakers in front of the shoal, and she turned on her side. She came over so hard that the ship's main engine was thrown through its side. She then broke longitudinally and the upper works, which held the victims, drifted downwind, sank, and was never seen again."

Two days later a tug was dispatched to search for the ship after it failed to arrive at its destination. On the shores of the Copperhead Islands, the crew found a metal lifeboat crushed at both ends, a lifejacket with the ship's name on it, and part of the ship's paddlebox revealing the letters WA. In 1880 the hull was finally discovered in the shallow water south of the Haystacks. Boaters still find remains of the *Waubuno* haunting the shoals of the bay to this very day.

To end the historic Spider Bay route, simply return to the access point on Three Legged Lake via the same route. With luck you will be able to count on the same wind from Georgian Bay that once battled against your bow, and use it to your advantage in sailing all the way to the eastern tip of Spider Lake.

**TIME** 2–5 days

**DIFFICULTY** Moderate tripping skills are needed to deal with the portage lengths into Clear Lake and heavy winds along the Spider Lake route.

**NUMBER OF PORTAGES** 4 (including 1 that has to be doubled back on) for the Clear Lake Loop and 1 (which must be doubled back on) for the Spider Lake route.

**LONGEST PORTAGE** 920 yards (840 m) (Clear Lake Loop)

**FEE** A fee is required for overnight camping, and permits can be obtained at Oastler Lake Provincial Park or Blackstone Harbour entry point.

**ALTERNATIVE ACCESS** It is possible to access the park at Blackstone Harbour. Turn east off Highway 400/69 onto Muskoka Road 11. Then, after the town of MacTier (almost 4 miles [6 km] from the highway), take the Healey and Kapikog Lake Road to reach the Petes Road and the Blackstone Harbour boat launch and fee station.

**ALTERNATIVE ROUTE** Both the Spider Lake route and Clear Lake Loop can be reached by making use of the Blackstone Harbour access point, located at the south end of the park.

**FISH SPECIES** Both the Clear Lake Loop and Spider Bay route offer excellent bass and pike fishing.

**KAYAK FRIENDLY** Long portages along the Clear Lake Loop make the route more suited for canoeists.

However, the Spider Lake route is perfect for kayaking.

**OUTFITTERS**
White Squall Wilderness Shop
R.R. 1
Nobel, Ontario
P0G 1G0
705-342-5324
or
19 James Street
Parry Sound, Ontario
P2A 1T4
705-746-4936
www.whitesquall.com

Swift Canoe & Kayak
(Georgian Bay)
Highway 400 North
Box 604
Waubaushene, Ontario
L0K 2C0
1-800-661-1429
georgianbay@swiftcanoe.com

**FOR MORE INFORMATION**
Massasauga Provincial Park
R.R. 2
Parry Sound, Ontario
P2A 2W8
reservations 1-888-668-7275
705-378-0685

Ministry of Natural Resources
Parry Sound District Office
7 Bay Street
Parry Sound, Ontario
P2A 1S4
705-746-4201

**MAPS** Massasauga Provincial Park has produced an excellent map of the park's interior.

**TOPOGRAPHIC MAPS**
41 H1, 41 H8 & 31 E4

# Muskoka
## A Rocky Place

**THE PIONEERS SETTLED IN THE MOMENT** they saw good stands of timber rooted into the Muskoka terrain. Back home, lush green forests were a clear indication of fertile soil for farming. Once they began to clear the mounds of ancient gneiss, however, they discovered only shallow soils carpeting an unworkable landscape. Their land of hopes and dreams soon looked like an unworkable landscape. Ultimately, it was the same trees that at first tricked the settlers into moving north to Muskoka that ended up being their saving grace. When the government granted timber licenses in the area, farmers exchanged their plows for axes and joined logging camps during the winter month to subsidize their unproductive farms.

This rocky fastness, which had to be given to the farmers free of charge before they would even think of settling, soon became the main attraction of Muskoka. Now the two-billion-year-old Canadian Shield draws people by the thousands. Exploring Muskoka by canoe is probably the best way to experience the ruggedness of this exposed landscape. There's something special about paddling Muskoka's sparkling lakes linked by historic waterways with tumbling waterfalls. Rocky shorelines thrust straight out of the water or roll out flat across the surface, and islands of pink granite look as if they are suspended in the morning mist. Muskoka is definitely a welcome mat placed at the entrance to the North for both cottagers and canoeists alike.

# Black River

**I REMEMBER MY FIRST NIGHT** along the banks of the Black. With my fire burning down to glowing embers, I felt the backwoods closing in and the darkness enhancing the illusion of wilderness solitude. In fact, if it hadn't been for the lights of an airplane flickering among the stars overhead, and the distant roar of traffic drowning out the cries of a gathering of whippoorwills, I could have sworn I was camped along a northern interior river rather than this south-central Ontario waterway.

The area surrounding the river has been developed, but it has managed to come through our onslaught generally unscathed. It's a natural area that has been preserved by sheer luck. For the past 400 years it has been known as the Forgotten Valley.

As early as the 1600s, the Hurons studiously avoided the waterway, fearing they would encounter raiding bands of Iroquois from upstate New York. In 1826, European surveyors chose to explore a communication link between the Ottawa River and Georgian Bay, via Lake Simcoe, by way of the southern branch of the Muskoka and the Madawaska River system. In the late 1800s, farmers found the mounds of gneiss on the river's shores of little value and left them for the loggers. The loggers took only the valley's pine, leaving the rest of the felled timber to rot. This made the landscape even more inhospitable for settlement. The discovery of what was thought to be gold almost caused a rush of development along the river, but the mineral was soon proven to be only fool's gold.

One of the main reasons for the protection of the Black was that for over 60 years a single block of land, including a part of the river system totaling 40 lakes, has been owned by an American company that has maintained it as a recreational reserve. So if you're looking for two days of wilderness tripping in the heart of cottage country, the Forgotten Valley of the Black is perfect.

Even though the river flows from just south of Dorset to Lake Simcoe, the best route is from Victoria Falls to Highway 169 (a distance of 18.5 miles [30 km]). Except in hot, dry summers, water levels allow you to travel the river right from break-up to freeze-up.

South of the town of Washago, the Black River flows under Highway 169. Park your second (pick-up) vehicle on the south side of the bridge in a clearing on the right side of the highway, next to the river. To reach the access point at Victoria Falls, drive toward Washago and turn right off Highway 169 onto Muskoka Street. Go through the town's business section. A few miles out of Washago, turn right onto Cooper's Falls Road (just after the bridge), heading

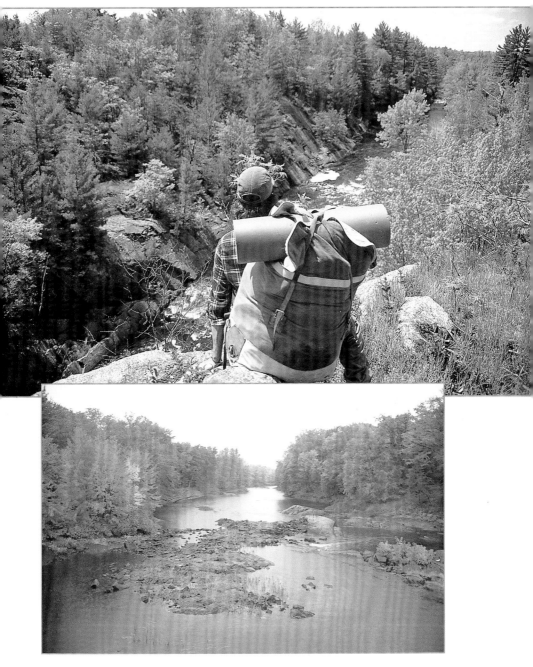

*Above: Taking a break on the portage around Ragged Rapids.*
*Below: Autumn on the Black River.*

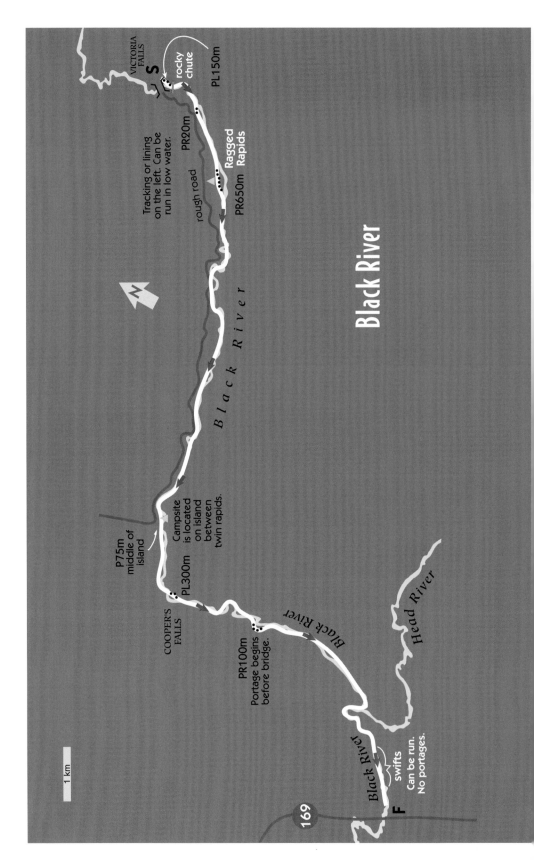

# Black River

1 km

N

VICTORIA FALLS

S

rocky chute

PL150m

Tracking or lining on the left. Can be run in low water.

PR20m

rough road

Ragged Rapids

PR650m

*Black River*

P75m middle of island

COOPER'S FALLS

PL300m

Campsite is located on island between twin rapids.

PR100m

Portage begins before bridge.

Black River

Head River

Black River

swifts
Can be run.
No portages.

F

169

toward the town of Cooper's Falls. Once at Cooper's Falls, remain on the paved road for 1.5 miles (2.5 km) east past the town and turn right onto a dirt road as it bends north toward Housey's Rapids. The narrow bush road, which runs next to the river at times, makes the almost 10 miles (14 km) to Victoria Falls seem twice as long, but eventually you will come to the bridge over the falls. Please note that no camping is allowed at the falls.

To put in, take the 165-yard (150 m) portage on the far side of the bridge and follow it down to a sandy beach at the base of Victoria Falls. Shortly after the put-in point, you are forced to either line your canoe or run a small, rocky chute. The run looks easy, but it's deceptive. To avoid having your canoe wedged broadside against a large boulder in midstream, it's best to choose to line your canoe down the cascading water. As you bypass the chute, keep an eye open for iron pegs anchored into the rocks. These are relics of the former Langford Lumber Company, which used to flush its logs down the Black.

Approximately 1.25 miles (2 km) downriver, you will come to a stunted falls. A 22-yard (20 m) portage is located along the right bank. During an early spring outing on the river, a friend from work, who had just happened to complete a whitewater workshop on the Madawaska River in Algonquin before our trip, decided to flush the canoe through the chute and down the thigh-high falls. Of course, I chose to jump out of the canoe and watch from shore. Everything went smoothly until he suddenly discovered how shallow the water was at the base of the falls. I cringed every time I heard the canoe crunch and grind along the rocky river bottom. Gertrude, my old beat-up fiberglass river canoe, escaped with only a little more paint scraped off her bow, but my companion faced an onslaught of teasing from yours truly for the rest of the day.

If you continue paddling for another 1.25 miles (2 km), you will come to one of the most scenic obstacles along the route. Ragged Rapids is impossible to run (even if you do go to whitewater workshops on the Madawaska) and can be avoided by using a 710-yard (650 m) portage that begins along the right bank well before the drop. The trail works its way up the steep bank to an old bush road. Follow the road over the top of the ridge and then go along the fork to the left, where the portage leads back to the river. This portage is the most difficult one on the route, not because of its length, but because of the muddy, slippery clay bank lined with patches of poison ivy at the trail's end.

Ragged Rapids, once home to a rural post office when a handful of settlers built shanties and squatted along the banks of the Black, is a great lunch spot. Open up your daypack and juice bottle either on top of the high ridge alongside the portage or clamber up onto the large rock pillar located midstream just before the rapids.

You can spend the afternoon paddling the slow-moving section of the river, where the Black's banks are a mixture of layered clay and sand. For birdwatchers, this quiet section is simply heaven. Thrushes blend in with the forest floor, rose-breasted grosbeaks sing among the upper canopy, woodcocks flush from patches of ostrich fern, and kingfishers and swallows burst from their nest holes in the exposed sand cliffs. If you are exploring the river in late May, make sure to tie your canoe up along shore now and then to investigate the dozens of wetland areas bordering the river. I once checked out a stand of dead snags and discovered one of the largest heron rookeries I've ever seen. High up in the trees, no fewer than 20 large stick structures swayed in the wind. Above the rookery, adult great blue herons homed in like planes at a busy airport. The moment I spotted young birds in the nests, I crept back to the river and paddled away from the wary parents.

The forest cover along the river varies from mixed conifer and deciduous trees to pure hardwood stands. One minute you think you're paddling through Southern Ontario woodlands of maple and birch, and the next you're venturing through the harsher conditions of Northern Ontario, characterized by its gnarled white pine and juniper bushes spreading across rocky knolls. With such varied forest cover, autumn can be an excellent season to travel down the Black and view the splendid fall colors.

Just when the meandering calm waters start to become a little monotonous, the river once again picks up its pace, creating double obstacles. The first is a short section of rapids that can easily be run, and the second, twin falls that go around either side of a small island and gush over scoured gneiss. An 80-yard (75 m) portage cuts through the middle of the island and ends at an excellent campsite along a sandy point with plenty of driftwood washed ashore to use as firewood. Set up your tent either on the exposed point or under the shade of the pines, then take a refreshing dip at the base of the falls.

A little over a mile (2 km) downriver you're forced to portage around Cooper's Falls via a 330-yard (300 m) portage to the left. If experience permits, you may want to run the set of rapids that rush under an old bridge just before the falls and take out before the drop. It's best, however, to portage around the entire section. If you ever capsized in the rapids, you would have an extremely bumpy ride ahead of you.

From Cooper's Falls the river slows down for approximately 5 miles (8 km), but is interrupted halfway by a single set of rapids that starts before another bridge. A rock garden at the base of the rapids make this section too difficult to run, so either use the 110-yard (100 m) portage along the right bank (beginning just before the bridge) or line your canoe down the series of shallow shelves.

While paddling the quiet waters once again, notice how on the left bank yellow birch, white pine, hemlock and Canada yew take root in rock, whereas on the right bank a totally opposite type of forest, composed of white birch, bur oak, basswood and three species of maple, grows from deep, rich soil.

The Black River eventually meets up with the Head River. The swampy sections at the junction make excellent waterfowl habitat. As you round a bend in the river, wood ducks and mergansers flush from cover, and muskrat scurry under protective overhangs. About a mile (less than 2 km) downstream, the river narrows and rock outcrops appear, creating a series of runnable swifts. Only just before Highway 169 does the river widen again, with birch, oak and maple dominating its banks.

After packing up your gear in your second vehicle, parked at the highway crossing, you will have reached the most difficult portion of the trip — the drive back to Victoria Falls down that bumpy, dusty dirt road.

# BLACK RIVER

**TIME** 1–2 days

**DIFFICULTY** No major rapids have to be navigated but moderate canoe tripping skills are necessary.

**NUMBER OF PORTAGES** 6

**LONGEST PORTAGE** 710 yards (650 m)

**FEE** The Black River is situated, for the most part, on Crown land, and no fee is needed for Canadian citizens.

**ALTERNATIVE ACCESS/ ALTERNATIVE ROUTE** The road to Victoria Falls is getting more difficult to drive and it may be a better option to access the river at the take-out point and paddle upstream, returning via the same route.

**FISH SPECIES** The upper section of the river is stocked with small brook trout, and small bass can be caught at the confluence of the Head River.

**KAYAK FRIENDLY** No

**OUTFITTERS**
SWIFT OUTFITTERS (MUSKOKA)
RR 1, Highway 11 North
Gravenhurst, Ontario
705-687-3710
muskoka@swiftcanoe.com

**FOR MORE INFORMATION**
MINISTRY OF NATURAL RESOURCES
Parry Sound District Office
7 Bay Street
Parry Sound, Ontario
P2A 1S4
705-746-4201

**TOPOGRAPHIC MAPS**
31 D/11 & 31 D/14

# South Branch Muskoka River

**ORIGINALLY THERE WERE ONLY TWO PATCHES** of Crown land along the entire stretch of the Muskoka River where canoeists could set up camp. The remaining shoreline was privately owned. It was next to impossible to paddle the full length (26 miles [42 km]) from Baysville to Bracebridge in a day. The Ministry of Natural Resources' Canoe Muskoka-Haliburton pamphlet suggests it was a two-day trip.

Recently, however, the town of Bracebridge, with the assistance of canoeist Murray Colarke, has developed three overnight spots about halfway between the two towns. The sites are specifically designed for canoeists who want to paddle the entire stretch but over a two-day period. Potential users are asked to contact the town of Bracebridge (705-645-5264) for directions to these sites.

To paddle this route, however, you still have to deal with the hassles of shuttling a vehicle, which is why one of the best ways to paddle the South Branch of the Muskoka River is to navigate it the old-fashioned way. After you paddle downstream from Baysville and camp at the Crown land campsites, turn around and battle the current upstream, just as the fur traders and explorers once did. I prefer this way. It gives you a true sense of history, paddling, poling and lining back up the river; you're using the canoe as a means of transportation through the wilderness and not just a recreational toy.

To reach the access point in the town of Baysville, either drive east along 117 from Highway 11 (north of Bracebridge) or drive west along 117 from Highway 35 (south of Dorset). A public access is located on the west side of the river below the dam in Baysville. The town of Baysville was once the southern terminal for steamships carrying freight and passengers around the Lake of Bays. And remaining from days gone by are two large, high docks, one on each side of the river, near the Highway 117 bridge.

The first portage (55 yards [50 m]), which bypasses Fair Falls, is situated almost a mile (1.5 km) from the put-in. (The only stretch of the river that may cause some difficulty lies between the falls and the second portage, which is approximately 1.25 miles [2 km] in length.) The river becomes narrow and you may have to line or simply wade the canoe through the shallows, especially on your return journey upstream. In low water make sure to use the channel to the left, which is approximately a quarter mile (0.4 km) from the base of Fair Falls.

Portage two is only 45 yards (41 m) in length and is located along the right bank. Almost 1.5 miles (2.5 km) from the portage the river splits, forming two islands (you may paddle either channel). Both these islands and the shoreline

*Early morning mist, Cooks Falls.*

opposite the islands are Crown land and camping is permitted here. You can, however, paddle farther downriver to Cooks Falls. Designated campsites are located above and below the falls. From your campsite, you can portage left of the falls 100 yards (91 m) and visit another scenic waterfall (a portage is on the right), where the river divides and then tumbles over the backbone of the Canadian Shield.

Falls such as these saved the Muskoka River from the same fate as the Trent and Severn Rivers, which were dredged to form the Trent-Severn waterway system. While at war with the United States in the early 19th century, the British military sought a water route between the St. Lawrence, Lake Ontario and Georgian Bay, which was considered safe from an American attack. Their two options were to build a canal, using either the Trent and Severn River systems, or to locate an unexplored waterway along the southern fringe of the Algonquin Dome. After several failed expeditions along the Muskoka–Madawaska River route, they finally chose the Trent Severn system.

Lieutenant Henry Briscoe was the first man to explore the Muskoka River (meaning he was the first to record his journey; Native trappers and hunters and a dozen or so fur traders used the river well before him). Briscoe's discovery in 1826 failed to excite the British military. The idea of a canal fell dead until entrepreneur Charles Shirreff arrived on the scene. Shirreff thought the route could be used as both a canal and a means of opening up vast areas for lumber and settlement. Shirreff's son, Alexander, explored the river in the early fall of 1829. After his journey, however, Alexander didn't see promise for both a canal and settlement in the Algonquin Dome. Thus the plans for a canal were dismissed.

The last and more noteworthy canal expeditions for the Algonquin Dome were completed by a famed explorer and mapmaker of the Canadian West, David Thompson. In 1837 the Legislative Assembly of Upper Canada ordered three surveys of the land between the Ottawa River and Lake Huron "to ascertain the nature of the country and to report the practicability of establishing a communication by Water between the same." Thompson was to survey the Muskoka–Madawaska route.

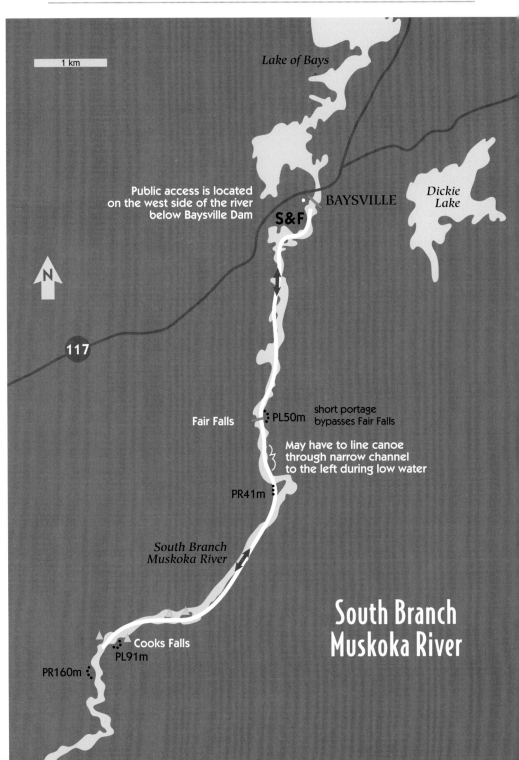

1 km

*Lake of Bays*

Public access is located
on the west side of the river
below Baysville Dam

**BAYSVILLE**

*Dickie
Lake*

**S&F**

N

117

Fair Falls    PL50m    short portage
bypasses Fair Falls

May have to line canoe
through narrow channel
to the left during low water

PR41m

*South Branch
Muskoka River*

**South Branch
Muskoka River**

Cooks Falls
PL91m

PR160m

Thompson's travels up the Muskoka never came close to his previous famous exploration of the Columbia River. He was 67 years old and lacked his youthful insight. Thompson agreed to the trip essentially because he needed the money. Nevertheless, his 100-page journal and maps of the route were far more detailed than those of the half-dozen expeditions before him combined.

Thompson questioned the building of a canal along the route well before he headed out, and once on the Muskoka he soon realized that the canal could never be established due to the river's endless falls and rapids. In fact, after pushing and dragging up through the same section of water you've just navigated down, Thompson noted that he and his companions had to stop "to dry again our Canoe, for it has suffered much on the Rocks and Stones coming up the Fall and Rapids and is now rather leaky."

Once handed over to the government, David Thompson's journal and maps were ignored and forgotten, and the great explorer died a poor man. His conclusion that a canal would be unfeasible still stands today — thank goodness.

During day two on the Muskoka, finish what you've started and take my advice by traveling against the current just as Thompson once did.

# SOUTH BRANCH MUSKOKA RIVER

**TIME** 1–2 days

**DIFFICULTY** A moderate level of experience is necessary, especially if you plan on lining upstream.

**NUMBER OF PORTAGES** 4 (all which must be doubled back on)

**LONGEST PORTAGE** 175 yards (160 m)

**FEE** The South Branch of the Muskoka River is situated, for the most part, on Crown land, and no fee is needed for Canadian citizens.

**ALTERNATIVE ACCESS/ ALTERNATIVE ROUTE** It is possible to access the river on the north side of Highway 118 and paddle upstream, returning via the same route.

**FISH SPECIES** The upper section of the river is stocked with small brook trout and small bass can be caught in the lower stretch.

**KAYAK FRIENDLY** No

**OUTFITTERS**
SWIFT OUTFITTERS (MUSKOKA)
RR 1, Highway 11 North
Gravenhurst, Ontario
1-800-661-1429
muskoka@swiftcanoe.com

**FOR MORE INFORMATION**
MINISTRY OF NATURAL RESOURCES
Bracebridge District Office
Box 1138
Bracebridge, Ontario
P0B 1C0
705-645-8747

**TOPOGRAPHIC MAP** 31 E/3

# Haliburton Highlands
## Accessible Wilderness

**LEGENDARY CANOEIST ERIC W. MORSE,** a man who became known as one of the few modern-day voyageurs, christened his paddle at the age of 12 in Haliburton. He wrote, "This was my eye-opening introduction to the Precambrian Shield. My own strong preference when canoeing is to travel in Precambrian terrain." In his lifetime, Morse traversed more rugged landscape than I could ever imagine, and he always remembered the spread of lakes and rockbound rivers in Haliburton's "accessible wilderness." That's one of the main attractions of the Highlands. Even after the government of Upper Canada constructed a road into Haliburton in 1859 for better access, this scenic land still remained somewhat wild.

Soon after it was founded in 1861, the Canadian Land and Emigration Company of London, England, purchased lands in the region for settlement. The town of Haliburton was surveyed in 1864, and a sawmill was erected that year; the following year saw the installation of a gristmill. Charles R. Stewart was appointed the first resident land agent, and the dream community was named in honor of judge and author Thomas Chandler Haliburton, chairman of the company, who never once set eyes on the highlands named after him.

Haliburton has changed somewhat over time. The land was first settled by farmers, but because the Highlands' rocky soil was unworkable, the cross-cut saw soon replaced the plow. Lumbering became a thriving business in Haliburton at the turn of the century and still remains profitable in some areas. Eventually tourism took hold.

The Highlands' wild splendor remained the magnet for people who desired solitude. The rolling landscape covered with stout pine, frothing rivers bordered by fantastic ruggedness, granite cliffs echoing the raven's cracking call, and deep lakes blanketed by morning mist attracted, and continue to attract, boaters and canoeists alike.

My season of paddling wouldn't be complete without a weekend trip through Leslie M. Frost's canoe routes or a run down the less-traveled Burnt River. Every year the Highlands casts its spell on me, dizzying my awareness of the outside world. You see, I too christened my paddle in Haliburton's Precambrian terrain, and I too will remember the spread of lakes and rockbound rivers in this "accessible wilderness."

# Leslie M. Frost Centre

Between 1892 and 1893, the Gilmour Lumber Company constructed an elaborate series of canals, dams and slides amid the Haliburton Highlands to transport logs over two heights of land and on to the company sawmill in Trenton. The costs for such a project forced the lumber enterprise to declare bankruptcy only two years later, with only one log drive ever reaching Trenton.

The crash of Gilmour Lumber Company and contributions from the Department of Lands and Forests (now Ontario Ministry of Natural Resources) made possible a 59,300-acre (24,000 ha) pocket of wilderness that still stands in sweet abandonment 7.5 miles (12 km) south of Dorset. The forest track is a paradise for canoeists, with dozens of maintained routes to choose from — free of charge. Here are four of my favorite two-day trips.

# St. Nora–Sherborne Lake

**THE FIRST ROUTE** can be reached directly from the Leslie M. Frost Natural Resource Centre, located along Highway 35 on the west shore of St. Nora Lake.

In the mid-1900s a training school for forest rangers was opened on the site of the present center. It ran until 1969, at which point it was closed. In 1974 it reopened as a center to educate the general public about forest management in Ontario. The center was named in honor of the late premier of Ontario, who was the first to perceive the need for such a facility. Today hundreds of tourists, schoolchildren and camp kids visit the center, and hundreds more head off into the expanse of public lands over which the Ministry of Natural Resources has custodianship.

A parking area is located between the main building and the reconstructed log cabin that was the first fire ranger cabin, built in 1929. In 1859 the site on which this cabin was later built was named Harvey's Landing by Francis Harvey, Dorset's first fur trader. Two of Harvey's children died of diphtheria and were buried to the left of the site. A monument was erected in 1967 in their memory.

To launch your canoe, use the dock on the public beach. To begin this route, paddle northeast from the dock, toward the picturesque St. Margaret Island. In the past, I've found that if there's a strong headwind it's best to keep to the left of the island, but paddling to the right is more direct.

St. Margaret Island was named after Mrs. Margaret Band. During the early spring of 1917, Margaret and several other women from the area lived in a log cabin while their men were off fighting in the Great War. They tapped the maple trees on the island and sent the maple sugar, marked "From St. Margaret Island," to their husbands overseas.

The island was also used as a graveyard for the local residents' dogs. When the pets grew old, Dr. Frain, the veterinarian, arrived from Minden by horse and buggy to chloroform them. They were then wrapped in Hudson's Bay blankets and buried in a dog cemetery with individual tombstones. The forget-me-nots that were planted on the gravesites still dot the island and can be seen as you glide by.

An interesting point to think about while paddling across St. Nora Lake is that you are actually crossing the 45th parallel, which means that you and your canoe are midway between the equator and the North Pole. The lake was originally called Sonora, a Native word for echoes, and became St. Nora when clumsily translated into English. If you doubt the aptness of the Native name for the lake, just call out and listen for the echo coming from the surrounding hills.

The first portage, which goes from St. Nora to Sherborne Lake, is located past St. Margaret Island, to the left of a shallow stream. The 890-yard (813 m) portage makes its way up a steep grade, then levels off, and you can either skirt the edge of a small pond or paddle across it. A boardwalk used to be in place here, making the first option the best. Now, however, you're sure to get your feet wet while walking across the mats of sphagnum and it's best to paddle across the pond. Whichever you choose, make sure to go right when you reach the main portage again, where it follows an old tote road to the Sherborne Dam.

Sherborne Lake (named after the township of Sherborne by which the lake resides) is engulfed by pronounced ridges of granite gneiss carpeted by stout white pine. The moment you exit the small west bay you will be greeted by the local gull population playing in the wind and merganser families hugging the weedy shoreline. Sherborne's wild inhabitants are an integrated bunch: the moose, traditionally a symbol of the North, can be found browsing in marshy bays, and the white-tailed deer, a more southern species, is often spotted in the adjacent forested valleys.

The large lake is sprinkled with forested islands to make camp on. Once you have selected a site, you can paddle off and explore some of the more secluded lakes nearby. An adventurous afternoon can be had northwest of Sherborne Lake paddling and portaging a loop connecting Sundew Pond, Little Avery Lake, Bruin Lake, Long Pond, Roche Pond, Plastic Lake and back to Sherborne. This trip is best done in early spring during high water. A hot summer spell can transform an enjoyable afternoon canoe trip into a bug-infested nightmare. I remember the first time I traveled this loop. It was during an extremely dry August, and I found myself less than 110 yards (100 m) from a bear while pulling my canoe through the knee-deep mud on Sundew Pond. The bear was preoccupied with a grub-filled log on top of a small rocky island, and I was concerned with the cloud of mosquitoes around my head, so neither of us bothered the other.

For the angler seeking a lake for the opening of trout season, Orley Lake, which can be accessed by a 280-yard (257 m) portage from Sherborne's north

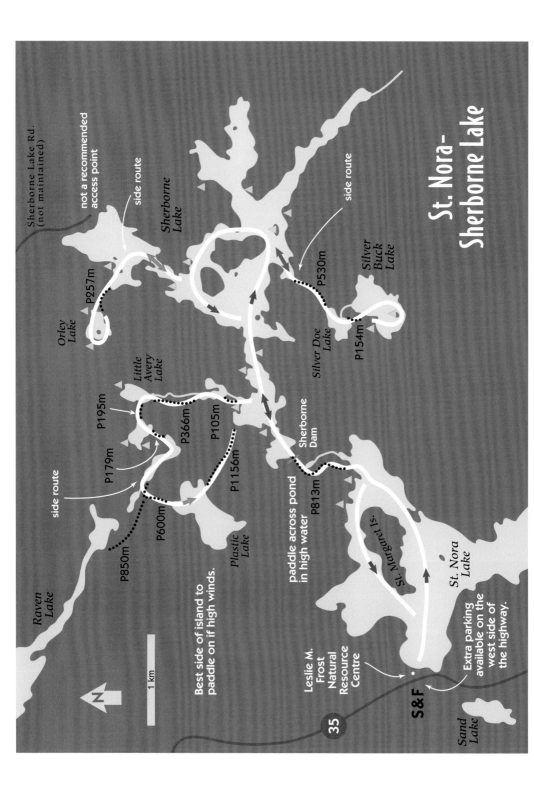

# St. Nora–Sherborne Lake

Sherborne Lake Rd.
(not maintained)

not a recommended
access point

side route

Sherborne
Lake

side route

P257m

Orley
Lake

Silver
Buck
Lake

P530m

P154m

Silver Doe
Lake

Little
Avery
Lake

P195m

P179m

P366m

P105m

P1156m

side route

P600m

P850m

Sherborne
Dam

P813m

Plastic
Lake

paddle across pond
in high water

Raven
Lake

St. Margaret Is.

St. Nora
Lake

Best side of island to
paddle on if high winds.

Leslie M.
Frost
Natural
Resource
Centre

Extra parking
available on the
west side of
the highway.

S&F

35

Sand
Lake

1 km

N

bay, is stocked with rainbow. If you prefer speckled trout, take the 580-yard (530 m) portage on Sherborne's south shore and either fish Silver Doe Lake or carry over into Silver Buck Lake. The small island located on Silver Buck makes an excellent spot to enjoy a shore lunch.

Sherborne is frequently used by summer camps in the area. It is great to come across a line of canoes filled with camp kids singing "Puff the Magic Dragon" or "Land of the Silver Birch." This place gives hundreds of children a wonderful sense of well-being. It's disheartening, however, to discover an abused campsite. While circling one of the islands on Sherborne in search of an unoccupied site, I witnessed half a dozen teenage girls washing their greasy dishes along the shoreline, then going to the same spot not ten minutes later to fill their water bottles. Fortunately, times are changing and groups who do not practice low-impact camping will soon be a thing of the past.

# ST. NORA–SHERBORNE LAKE

**TIME** 2 days

**DIFFICULTY** This is a perfect novice trip.

**NUMBER OF PORTAGES** 1

**LONGEST PORTAGE** 890 yards (813 m)

**FEE** The route is situated in the Leslie M. Frost Centre, where no fees are required.

**ALTERNATIVE ACCESS** Sherborne Lake can be accessed directly by a rough dirt road just north of the Frost Centre, on the east side of Highway 35. Take note, however, that driving the road is not recommended.

**ALTERNATIVE ROUTE** A number of side routes (Silver Buck Lake, Orley Lake and the Plastic Lake Loop) are possible from Sherborne Lake.

**FISH SPECIES** St. Nora and Sherborne Lakes offer fair fishing for lake trout and bass. Orley Lake is stocked with rainbow trout, and Silver Doe and Silver Buck are stocked with brook trout.

**KAYAK FRIENDLY** Yes (it's possible to use a wheel cart to transport kayak over that long portage).

**OUTFITTERS** None

**FOR MORE INFORMATION**
LESLIE M. FROST CENTRE
R.R. 2
Minden, Ontario K0M 2K0
705-766-2451

MINISTRY OF NATURAL RESOURCES
Minden District Office
Minden, Ontario K0M 2K0
705-286-1521

**MAPS** Chrismar Mapping Co. has produced an excellent map detailing the interior canoe routes of the Leslie M. Frost Centre.

**TOPOGRAPHIC MAP** 31 E/2

# McKewen Lake Loop

**AT TIMES IT'S BEST TO AVOID THE CROWDS** east of Highway 36 and paddle the western chain of lakes. The McKewen Lake Loop is a perfect answer to escaping the line-ups for the Sherborne portage and has the virtue of being accessible from the highway bridge at Wren Lake, just north of the Frost Centre.

It's possible to access Margaret Lake directly, using Margaret Lake Road, west of Highway 35, but the Wren Lake access makes for a much better trip. Make use of the parking area on the east side of the highway, north of the bridge. From here, put in on Wren Lake and paddle southwest. Eventually you'll come to the shallows, where a 250-yard (228 m) portage is marked to the right. You can either take the portage or, if water levels permit, lift over the island in the middle of the narrows, then take the tail end of the portage to the base of the falls. Beware while crossing this area, for it is said to be cursed by the men who died mysteriously in the 1830s while surveying and building the historic Bobcaygeon Road that once crossed here.

From the falls follow the narrow channel, matted with lily pads, to the next portage (370 yards [337 m]), marked to the left of the rapids.

Again, push your canoe through a wetland valley. A few years ago, while paddling through this lower marsh, I spotted a water shrew running along the top of the water. Like a water strider (a spiderlike insect), this aquatic shrew is able to "walk" on water because of the tiny air bubbles trapped between its toes, which keep them from breaking the surface tension of the water. On the same trip, I mistakenly spooked a moose who was browsing on water plants. The large bull ran up onto the shore, climbed up the slippery bank, shook his damp fur and flung a haze of spray into the air, then quickly disappeared into the forest, leaving me alone in awe.

Halfway along the lower marsh to the left is the 250-yard (228 m) portage to Horse Lake. A wooden dock sticks out from the muddy shore to help keep your feet dry while beaching your canoe. The pathway begins almost immediately with a steep incline, taking you over the height of land where the waters behind you flow to the west into Georgian Bay, and the waters over the rise flow south into the Trent system.

Horse Lake is a quick paddle with a nice lunch island halfway across. At the south end of this lake, there is a 228-yard (208 m) portage leading you into McKewen Lake. This lake, named after the former director of the Frost Centre's ranger school, is the best place to make camp. With the afternoon still ahead of

*Above: Granite cliffs and stout white pine are among Haliburton's main attractions (Sherborne Lake). Below: Taking in the scenery — a cow moose with calf — on Horse Lake.*

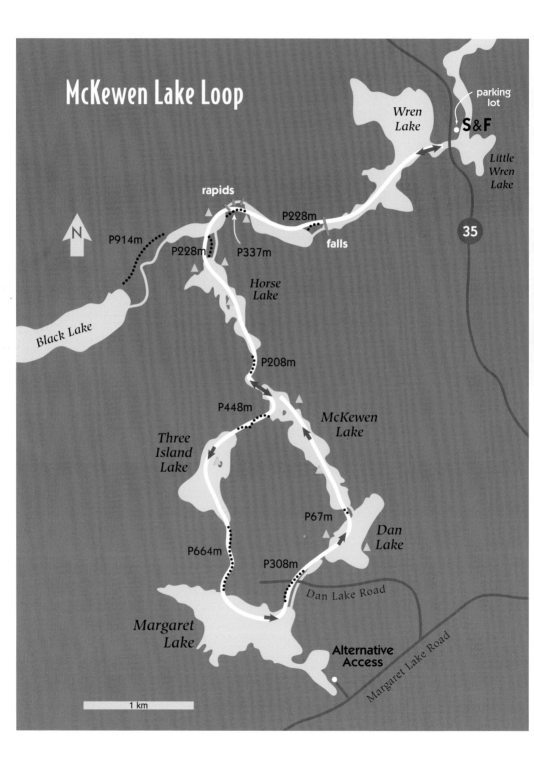

# McKewen Lake Loop

Wren Lake

parking lot

**S & F**

Little Wren Lake

35

**rapids**

N

P914m

P228m

P337m

P228m

**falls**

Horse Lake

Black Lake

P208m

P448m

McKewen Lake

Three Island Lake

P67m

Dan Lake

P664m

P308m

Dan Lake Road

Margaret Lake

**Alternative Access**

Margaret Lake Road

1 km

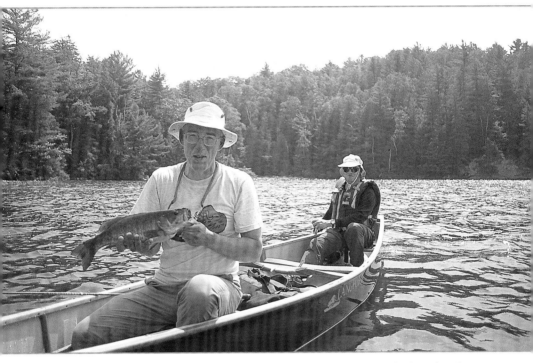

*Canoeists from the Durham Outdoors Club take time out to catch shore lunch (Margaret Lake).*

you, however, why not paddle the Three Island Lake–Margaret Lake–Dam Lake Loop before choosing your site. If you decide to spend the afternoon traveling the loop, take the 490-yard (448 m) portage to Three Island Lake, found just a quarter of the way down McKewen Lake on the western shore, almost directly behind the small island.

If you decide it is too early to break open the lunch pack on Horse Lake, the third islet on Three Island Lake is a good second choice. The next portage, the 726 yards (664 m) to Margaret Lake, to the south of Three Island Lake, is a relatively flat pathway through a woodland dominated by beech, oak and maple. You will find that most of the surrounding forest is made up of 30-to-40-year-old hardwood stands. This second growth took over the area after the Gilmour lumbermen cleared the white spruce to use as fuel in the company's jackladder boilers, which transported logs from lake to lake. Gilmour Lumber built a giant tramway to move logs over the height of land between Lake of Bays and St. Nora Lake. The distance was only just over 6 miles (10 km), but the tramway cost over $10 million to construct.

After reaching Margaret Lake, paddle east, hugging the north shore until you reach the 337-yard (308 m) portage to Dan Lake. The bay that opens up into Dan Lake is cluttered with a maze of dead snags that resemble ghostly statues. The dead trees are vital for nesting birds, and swallows can often be seen flying from these natural high-rise hotels to snatch bugs from the air. Once you navigate through the swampy bay, there is an inviting campsite directly to the east. You can either pitch your tent here or, as I have previously mentioned, finish the loop by way of a 73-yard (67 m) portage to the west, into McKewen Lake. Of McKewen's two main campsites, the more attractive is on the north end; it is situated on a point of land to the east (directly across from the portage into Three Island Lake) and has an ideal rock where you can sit and watch the sun set.

The next day return via familiar Horse Lake, Black River and Wren Lake, thus ending a perfect two-day trip.

## MCKEWEN LAKE LOOP

**TIME** 2 days

**DIFFICULTY** Moderate level of canoe tripping is needed.

**NUMBER OF PORTAGES** 8 (4 of which must be doubled back on)

**LONGEST PORTAGE** 726 yards (664 m)

**FEE** The route is situated in the Leslie M. Frost Centre, where no fees are required.

**ALTERNATIVE ACCESS** Margaret Lake public launch, located west off Highway 35 on Margaret Lake Road.

**ALTERNATIVE ROUTE** By using the Margaret Lake access point, the entire section of Black River and Horse Lake can be eliminated.

**FISH SPECIES** McKewen, Dan and Horse Lakes are stocked with splake. Wren Lake and Margaret Lake have a small population of lake trout and both offer good fishing for bass.

**KAYAK FRIENDLY** No

**OUTFITTERS** None

**FOR MORE INFORMATION**
LESLIE M. FROST CENTRE
R.R. 2
Minden, Ontario
K0M 2K0
705-766-2451

MINISTRY OF NATURAL RESOURCES
Minden District Office
Minden, Ontario
K0M 2K0
705-286-1521

**MAPS** Chrismar Mapping Co. has produced an excellent map detailing the interior canoe routes of the Leslie M. Frost Centre.

**TOPOGRAPHIC MAP** 31E/2

# Herb and Gun Lakes

**CANADA'S GURU OF CANOEING,** the late Bill Mason, once remarked that "anybody who tells you portaging is fun has got to be a liar or is crazy." Consequently, I feel like I'm in good company when I get the urge to spend two days on the water, portage-free.

Herb Lake, situated in the more isolated northern section of Leslie M. Frost's Forest Reserve, is perfect for such a hassle-free holiday. One can easily have an enjoyable wilderness weekend by simply putting in at the Ministry of Natural Resources access point, paddling to one of the maintained sites on Herb Lake, and then spending the rest of the time swimming, fishing or just relaxing. If you are willing to strap a daypack on your back and balance the canoe on your shoulders across a few short portages, you can also spend your time visiting the small scenic lakes surrounding the area, such as Bull, Cow, Knife and Ronald Lakes.

The Herb Lake access point can be reached by turning right off Highway 35 onto Kawagama Road (No. 8), just north of the town of Dorset. At the first junction, turn right onto No. 8 (the continuation of Kawagama Road) and when the road forks, turn to your right. Halfway along the road (approximately 6.5 miles, or 11 km), just past Minden Bay, turn right again onto the dirt road leading to Herb Lake. Herb Lake Road is not marked, and I have driven straight past it many times. It helps to note that the dirt road is a little more than 1.25 miles (2.2 km) west of Deer Bay Road, which is marked. Parking is available for at least five vehicles.

Several forest fires swept through the Frost Centre lands back in 1867, 1875, 1915 and 1920. The blackened granite and fire scars are especially noticeable in the Herb Lake area. Due to the past burn-over, jack pine dominate large sections of the rocky landscape. This needle-leafed tree is well adapted to areas affected by forest fires. The jack pine holds seeds in its cones, and these are sealed by resin. High temperatures caused by fire melt the resin seal and disperse the seeds onto enriched blackened soil. Because few competitors survive fires, the sun-loving conifer does quite well. White and red pine have also reestablished themselves in patches, as well as pioneer species such as poplar and white birch.

If you're visiting the area between mid-July and mid-August, make sure to take time out to climb the exposed ridges and pick a bucketful of blueberries. There really is nothing as satisfying as fresh blueberry pancakes for breakfast.

If you do end up feeling a little more adventurous and wish to explore further ground to heighten your wilderness experience, a longer route can be taken into Gun Lake.

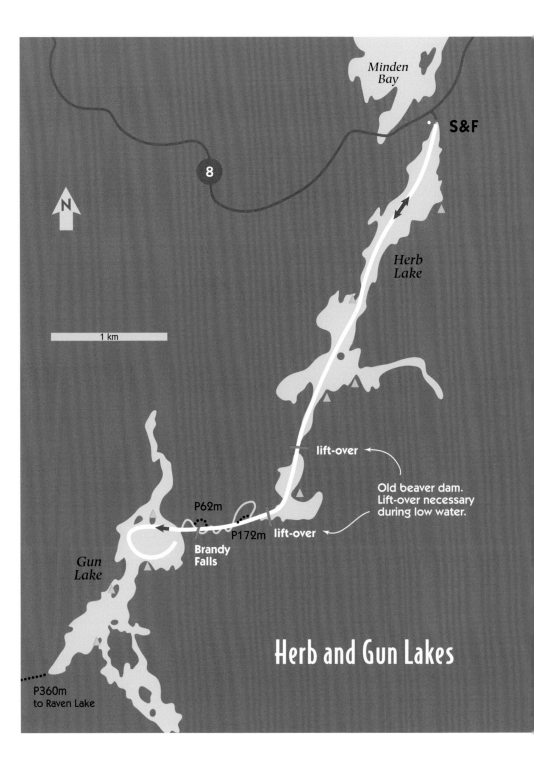

Minden
Bay

**S&F**

8

N

1 km

Herb
Lake

lift-over

Old beaver dam.
Lift-over necessary
during low water.

P62m

P172m    lift-over

Brandy
Falls

Gun
Lake

## Herb and Gun Lakes

P360m
to Raven Lake

*One of the good things about fall paddling: no bugs (Herb Lake).*

Paddle the length of Herb Lake and adjoining Ernest Lake, and follow the Black River connecting Ernest and Gun Lakes. The river's mouth is located at the far southwestern bay of Ernest Lake. Two short portages (188 yards and 68 yards [172 m, 62 m]) are marked first along the left bank, then on the right bank of the river; these circumvent two sets of falls. If water levels are low and beavers are active in the area, you may have to complete a lift-over or two en route. Excellent island campsites can be found on the more isolated Gun Lake, along with weedy bays where you might spot a moose nibbling on aquatic plants or hook into a meaty bass for dinner.

The last time I canoed along this route, the lakes were covered in ice and snow. During winter months I have often traded in my canoe and paddle for skis and snowshoes to continue traveling the canoe routes of cottage country. Admittedly, there are a number of hazards that go along with trekking through a frozen landscape: crossing muskeg swamps and having to check for thin ice while traveling on frozen rivers, to name just two. Winter portages are marked throughout the Frost Centre property, however, and if you keep to the groomed trails, exploring Haliburton's winter wonderland can be quite safe. Besides, there is one advantage to skiing or snowshoeing across the same lakes you canoed on during the summer months — no bugs!

Should you use skis or snowshoes? Well, cross-country skis will get you to your campsite more quickly, but I find it difficult enough balancing myself along the well-groomed trails, let alone bushwhacking with a 60-pound pack. Snowshoes will make you float over the 3 to 6 feet (1–2 m) of snow with ease, but your ankles and upper-thigh muscles will ache at the day's end. Combining both modes of travel is my choice.

Cooking stoves are essential. Don't even think about boiling up dinner on a blazing fire. By the time you reach camp, you will be too hungry to wait for dinner to cook on an open fire. Remember as well that your food is mainly what keeps you warm. So fill your recipes with generous amounts of calories. Take it easy on the spices, though. If you think it's a displeasure squatting in the backwoods to relieve yourself during the summer, just imagine what it's like during the winter.

I could go on listing the necessities required to survive a winter expedition and the attendant advantages and disadvantages of such an outing. However, the only additional thing you need is a love of solitude. It's not the cold temperatures, deep snow or distinct challenge that lures me out into the sleeping wilds. It's the beauty of its peaceful wilderness slumber.

## HERB AND GUN LAKES

**TIME** 1–2 days

**DIFFICULTY** This is a perfect novice route.

**NUMBER OF PORTAGES** 2 (both of which must be doubled back on)

**LONGEST PORTAGE** 188 yards (172 m)

**FEE** The route is situated in the Leslie M. Frost Centre, where no fees are required

**ALTERNATIVE ACCESS** Raven Lake public boat launch, east of Highway 35.

**ALTERNATIVE ROUTE** It's possible to portage into Gun Lake from Raven Lake.

**FISH SPECIES** Herb and Gun Lakes provide good bass fishing.

**KAYAK FRIENDLY** Yes, especially Herb Lake

**OUTFITTERS** None

**FOR MORE INFORMATION** LESLIE M. FROST CENTRE R.R. 2 Minden, Ontario K0M 2K0 705-766-2451

MINISTRY OF NATURAL RESOURCES Minden District Office Minden, Ontario K0M 2K0 705-286-1521

**MAPS** Chrismar Mapping Co. has produced an excellent map detailing the interior canoe routes of the Leslie M. Frost Centre.

**TOPOGRAPHIC MAP** 31 E/2

# Nunikani Loop

**BACK IN MY HIGH-SCHOOL DAYS,** a few classmates and I would gather every weekend to take a canoe trip. After graduation, however, we all went our separate ways, and I was the only one who continued the quest for great outdoor adventures.

Now that all my chums have grabbed hold of steady jobs, and some are even married and have children, we rekindle the old days by gathering once a year to go back in time, with paddles in hand. During the spring of 1992, I guided our group to one of my favorite lakes, Nunikani, set among the wilds of the Haliburton Highlands. After that memorable weekend we all decided that the '92 canoe trip had been one of the best reunions, and once you have tried the Nunikani Loop you will know why.

To reach the access point on Big Hawk Lake, follow Highway 35 north toward Dorset. Just past Halls Lake, turn right onto Road 13 and then left on Big Hawk Road. The paved road turns to dust and dirt halfway along, and at the dam on the Kennisis River you can view the historic log sluiceway. To put in, park your vehicle near the marina and push off from the beach to the left of the bridge, then paddle the length of the southwestern inlet and go around to the right, into Big Hawk Lake.

When canoeing the Nunikani Loop, I prefer to make the first day the longest and so head northeast, traveling counterclockwise. To reach the first portage, paddle the length of Big Hawk, keeping to the left inlet. Near the end of the far north-eastern inlet (Little Clear Lake), along the western shoreline, a relatively flat 250-yard (225 m) portage into Clear Lake is marked. Clear Lake is exactly that — clear. Its waters give off a turquoise glow at the surface, and the lake's bottom frequently flashes under your canoe, creating an effect that is quite dizzying and transfixing.

To reach the next portage, paddle out of the long inlet and then go straight across Clear Lake to the north shore. You have a choice of two paths (220 yards or 300 yards [200 m or 276 m]), both leading to Red Pine Lake. The longer portage on the right is only used when the middle section of the trail to the left becomes wet and muddy.

Red Pine is another big lake, and many canoeists choose to camp on its three large islands. The sites are scenic but a bit overused for my liking. It is also the place where I once witnessed a horrifying example of the future of recreational canoe-tripping.

While traveling across Red Pine Lake, I met the Joneses, a well-off city couple who were out on their first canoe trip. I couldn't help but notice that they were

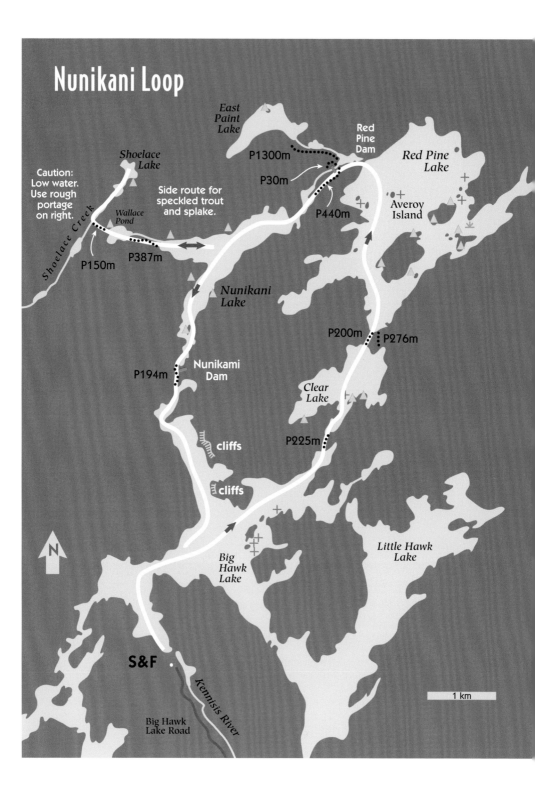

# Nunikani Loop

East Paint Lake

Shoelace Lake

Red Pine Dam

Red Pine Lake

P1300m

P30m

Caution: Low water. Use rough portage on right.

Side route for speckled trout and splake.

Wallace Pond

Averoy Island

P440m

P150m

P387m

Nunikani Lake

P200m  P276m

P194m

Nunikami Dam

Clear Lake

cliffs

P225m

cliffs

N

Little Hawk Lake

Big Hawk Lake

S&F

Kennisis River

1 km

Big Hawk Lake Road

equipped with every bit of paraphernalia imaginable. The only thing missing was common sense.

I introduced myself to Mr. and Mrs. Jones while they ate brunch from a plastic foldout picnic table on the island site where I had planned to make camp. I was forced to settle for second best — a site located in the center of a lowland swamp.

After I had set up my tent on a small mound of rock, my neighbors called me over for coffee. I eagerly jumped into my canoe and paddled to the Joneses' place. During my visit Mr. Jones showed off the camping toys he had purchased for their first-time wilderness adventure. Apart from the necessities — air mattresses, a Coleman stove and lantern, a six-person dome-style tent and a portable picnic table — the Joneses had brought along two large coolers to hold milk, steak, eggs and three bottles of bubbly; a large boombox complete with compact disc player (Dan Gibson's sounds of nature CDs cluttered the site); and even solar-powered transmitters that sounded the hunting cry of the mosquito's worst enemy, the dragonfly. For their reading pleasure, they had procured large hardcover copies of Bill Mason's books, *Path of the Paddle* and *Song of the Paddle*. They had also brought both a hand axe and bowsaw for cutting firewood. (I honestly looked around for the chainsaw.) I gulped down my coffee (with Irish Cream) and paddled back to my tiny tent to cook a pot of freeze-dried stew, feeling, quite frankly, a little envious.

The next morning I headed out on the water extra early. As I pulled up to the beginning of the portage into Nunikani Lake, I recognized a large pile of designer camping gear. I figured the only way Mr. and Mrs. Jones could have started off before me was with the help of their battery-operated alarm clock. I quickly put my rustic pack on my back, flipped Gertrude, my faithful 14-foot fibreglass canoe, onto my shoulders and trotted down the portage.

A few minutes later I heard the Joneses bickering up ahead on the trail. "It was your idea to buy this 18-foot canoe," Mrs. Jones insisted. "Well it was your idea to lash the picnic table inside it," Mr. Jones replied.

As you have probably already guessed, I now prefer to stay overnight on the more isolated Nunikani Lake. It's one of my favorite lakes in the Leslie Frost Forest Reserve. To reach it from Red Pine, follow the western shoreline to the little channel directly across from small Averoy Island. Take out to the right of the dam and either cross over and take the 480-yard (440 m) portage, following the left bank of the Kennisis River, or, if water levels permit and a little foam and froth doesn't scare you, simply lift over to the base of the cement structure and navigate your canoe down a short set of rapids. Make sure to stay clear of the tumbling water below the dam; the current is extremely powerful there. It's best to get your feet wet and wade your canoe down the right fork of the rapids.

*It's hard to believe we've survived more than 14 years of paddling together (Nunikani Lake).*

In early spring, this section of fast water is clogged with lake suckers spawning on the riverbed. And during the summer months, the shoreline is decorated with a diversity of flora and fauna. Hummingbirds hum around the dark red cardinal flowers, and tiny wrens bounce across the shrubs that overhang the banks.

Nunikani's northern bay is cluttered with stumps and reeds, an excellent place to fish for bass with surface plugs come nightfall, but first make camp at one of the five designated sites. My favorite is on the northwest point. The camp is set among a neck of pines facing a rock slab, which is great for swimming or catching a breeze to keep the mosquitoes at bay.

This was the site my friends and I chose as a base camp during our 1992 spring trip. After a couple of years of guiding them to the more hard-to-get-to lakes, I decided to take them on this less strenuous route. I assured them that they would be able to pack a few luxuries (not as many as the Joneses, of course). So instead of bringing freeze-dried stew, they brought frozen steaks, and Mike, the camp cook, was even allowed to pack a grill for the fire. We also equipped ourselves with a wide assortment of lines and tackle in the hope of having fish for breakfast. Of course, who would have thought that a group of enthusiastic anglers would forget the most essential item. You guessed it — we left the landing net at home. Nobody really seemed too concerned about this because we didn't really think we would catch any fish. We never had on any of our other trips. But the moment we portaged into Wallace Pond, a small lake to the west of Nunikani that can be reached via a rugged 425-yard (387 m) portage, we were shocked to see speckled trout darting at our shiny lures. (Take note that splake are now the species stocked in Wallace Pond.)

Most of the fish were pan-sized, so we simply flipped the trout onto the lap of our non-fishing canoe partner. Then Doug, a man who knows more about dividends and decimal points than the art of angling, hooked onto a trophy-size brookie. Now you might think that reeling in the biggest fish of the day from an overloaded canoe would make a banker a bit tense. Not really. In fact, Doug's canoe partner, the camp cook, was a tad more nervous than he. You see it was up to Mike to land the huge fish. I guess all of us yelling directions didn't ease the situation, especially when we burst out laughing the moment Mike grabbed for the fish and let the two-pound speckled slip through his grip. Doug didn't speak to Mike for a good part of the day, and we continued to drill him about remembering to bring a grill but not a net for the fish. The two anglers even headed out just before dark to try to catch the trout again, only to return empty-handed and swollen from bug bites.

By the next day, things had settled down a little. In fact, we didn't even tease Mike; that is, until he suggested we troll while paddling across Nunikani on the way home so that Doug could catch another wall-hanger. It didn't take long before, believe it or not, Doug hooked into another trophy fish — this time a huge laker. We gathered around their canoe to watch the antics of the banker and the cook once again. While Doug wrestled with the fish, we all offered to help Mike land it, but he insisted we allow him to regain his friendship with Doug and land the catch by himself.

After a good 20-minute fight, Doug pulled the lake trout alongside the canoe and again his catch slipped through Mike's fingers. The prospects for restoring their friendship looked bleak. Only 10 minutes later, however, Doug hooked onto yet another laker. This time, as we approached their canoe to watch, nobody said a thing. It was as if we were a losing baseball team. We needed a home run to win and Butterfingers Mike was up to bat. As the fish swam alongside the canoe, Doug broke the silence by whispering to Mike, "Three strikes and you're out, Mike — out of the boat, that is." Mike grabbed a frying pan from his pack, quickly placed it under the lake trout and flipped the fish, which was too big for the pan, into Doug's lap. We cheered while Mike and Doug, now best of friends, yelled, "Home run!"

To head back to Big Hawk Lake and the marina where your vehicle is parked, take the 212-yard (194 m) portage from the southern end of Nunikani Lake at the dam, following the right bank of the Kennisis River to the far northwestern inlet of Big Hawk Lake. Keep to the shoreline to your right. On your way along the western inlet, take note of the cliffs to your left. According to legend, one of the area's pioneers befriended a Native and was repaid with instructions as to the location of a hidden gold mine. However, the pioneer was unable to find it. Having read about the landmarks (two pines prominently situated on a mountain), I would guess the gold is somewhere on top of those cliffs.

At the mouth of the western inlet, keep following the shoreline to your right until you get to where the lake narrows; then paddle south, down the familiar inlet toward the marina and bridge. You will now have completed one of the best weekend loops in Haliburton.

# NUNIKANI LOOP

**TIME** 2 days

**DIFFICULTY** A moderate level of canoe-tripping experience is needed.

**NUMBER OF PORTAGES** 4

**LONGEST PORTAGE** 480 yards (440 m) (used only during low water levels)

**FEE** The route is situated in the Leslie M. Frost Centre, where no fees are required.

**ALTERNATIVE ACCESS** A public boat launch can be used at the Red Pine Lake Dam, reached by driving the Kennisis Lake Road.

**ALTERNATIVE ROUTE** Wallace Pond, reached by portaging in from the west end of Nunikani Lake, makes a great side route. It is also possible to paddle/portage in and out of Nunikani Lake from the Big Hawk access point.

**FISH SPECIES** Big Hawk, Little Hawk and Nunikani Lakes have fair lake trout and bass fishing; Clear Lake has a good population of lake trout; East Paint Lake and Wallace Pond are stocked with splake; and Wallace Pond and Shoe Lace Lakes offer good speckle trout fishing.

**KAYAK FRIENDLY** No

**OUTFITTERS** None

**FOR MORE INFORMATION**
LESLIE M. FROST CENTRE
R.R. 2
Minden, Ontario
K0M 2K0
705-766-2451

MINISTRY OF NATURAL RESOURCES
Minden District Office
Minden, Ontario
K0M 2K0
705-286-1521

**MAPS** Chrismar Mapping Co. has produced an excellent map detailing the interior canoe routes of the Leslie M. Frost Centre.

**TOPOGRAPHIC MAP** 31 E/2

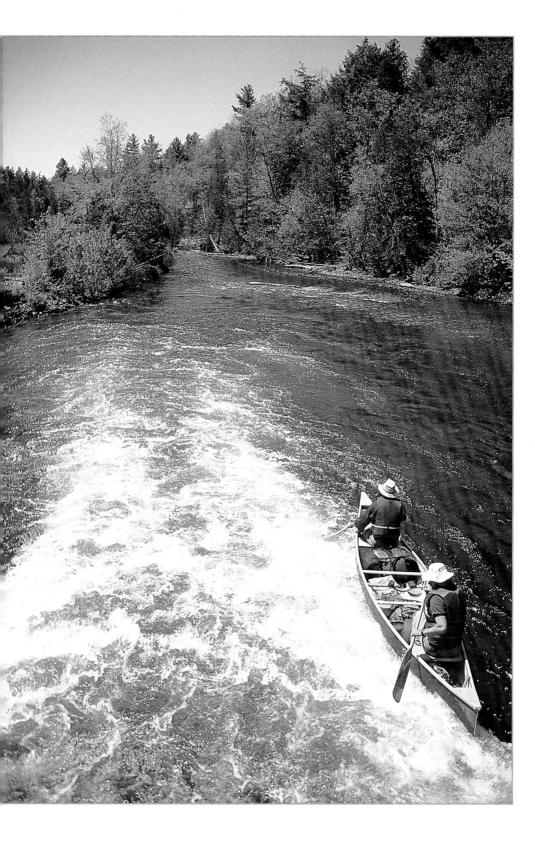

# Black Lake Loop

**IT WAS BRIAN REID WHO INITIATED MY WRITING CAREER.** He was the editor of my hometown newspaper, the *Milton Observer*, and needed an outdoor column for the weekly paper. Fresh out of college, I could hardly classify myself as an experienced writer, but with dozens of outdoor adventures behind me, I made a perfect anecdotist for Brian's newspaper. Over the years, we have become friends and paddling partners. We've spent many a day on the water together and many a night sharing a bottle of brandy around the campfire. Our most memorable trip was the one we took through the Black Lake Loop.

We set out early on a Saturday morning in June, driving north of Minden on Highway 35. Instead of leaving our vehicle at the parking lot alongside Raven Lake, east of the highway, we turned left up a township road to Shoe Lake. Many canoeists park at Raven Lake and portage over 1,200 yards (1,100 m) to Shoe Lake, not realizing that there is room available for at least five vehicles at Shoe Lake's municipal parking area.

The shoreline of Shoe Lake was lined with flowering purple pickerel weed and rustic cottages, each with a beached wood and canvas canoe. As Brian and I made our way across the lake, a family of loons swam up to the canoe to welcome us.

Reality set in as we attempted the first portage, 1,200 yards (1,097 m) in length. We traveled left along a dirt road and shortly after took a sharp right into the bush. The poorly marked trail became confusing when it forked, but we kept to the right and soon followed a well-worn portage through stands of maple and beech.

The moment we glimpsed Blue Chalk Lake's glistening turquoise water, we understood why the locals prefer to call it Clear Lake. A 50-yard (46 m) portage, which is located in the southern bay of Blue Chalk and works its way over a private cottage access road, took us into Red Chalk Lake. Here 17 mergansers greeted us in a shallow, narrow channel. The portage connecting Red Chalk Lake to Skeleton (Carcass) Lake was a challenge to find. But by paddling straight across from the narrow channel (keeping between the two points of land) and searching the shoreline to our left, we finally located the rolling, rugged 500-yard (457 m) trail.

A slight drizzle hung over Skeleton Lake as Brian and I set our paddles down and prepared lunch out in the middle of the small lake. As I sliced some bread and cheese, he tossed a surface lure toward shore and landed a four-pound largemouth bass. Enticed by his catch, I grabbed my rod and reel and we both tried our luck in a weedy bay to the south.

After fishing the bay, we finished our lunch at a designated campsite located along the eastern shore at the beginning of the 900 yard (823 m) portage to

*Brian captures the rewards of an early-morning paddle on Raven Lake.*

Upper Pairo (Twin) Lake. With full bellies we carried our equipment over the relatively flat path, which made its way through a thick stand of conifers, then twisted around a swampy meadow. After that we went up and down a number of hilly knolls to yet another small lake.

We wet our lines once again in Upper Pairo Lake, and this time I pulled in a hefty smallmouth bass. With such excellent fishing, we almost opted to stay at a nice campsite along the northeast shoreline, nestled among some soft pines, but at the last minute we decided to continue toward Black Lake.

The next portage, crossing over into Lower Pairo (Twin) Lake, was an easy 150 yards (137 m). Again the lake had the same characteristics as the former bodies of water, except for a gathering of anglers who were lowering their outboards at the road access located across the way. Watching the boats whiz toward us, Brian and I stood bewildered, feeling a little silly that we had worked our way through the bush all morning only to circle back to another public access point. What was worse was that we were forced to paddle past the fishermen's elaborate campsite, begin a lengthy 1,600-yard (1,463 m) portage at a parking lot, then wend our way up a dusty road. Only when we came to a rise on a steep grade and followed a sign to the left, which told us to leave the road and return to the bush, did we seem to be on track again. (Take note that this trail can be difficult to locate in some areas due to the recent logging activity, and care should be taken to keep on the right path.)

The portage finally made its way back to water by taking us through a logging site and then down the bank of the Black River. At first we lost the path in a field, but by heading across the opening we accidentally came upon a snowmobile trail running parallel to the river. The water level was down, forcing us to put in at the portage and load up our packs farther upriver toward Black Lake.

The clouds had teased us throughout the day, and by the time we paddled out of the river's weedy mouth and into the large lake, we were finally forced to

# Black Lake Loop

N

1 km

Raven Lake

Raven's Cliff

Alternative Start and Finish

Little Wren Lake

P46m

Raven Lake Dam

35

Five Mile Bay

Wren Lake

falls

Alternative Start and Finish

P228m

Grindstone Lake

rapids

P337m

P1189m

Portage follows along Township Rd.

S&F

falls

P914m

Shoe Lake

Black Lake

P1097m

Logging site
*Trail difficult to locate through logging site.

Blue Chalk Lake

P1463m

P46m

Red Chalk Lake

P137m

P457m

Carcass Lake

P823m

Pairo Lakes

Portage follows along dirt road for a short distance.

unpack our rain gear. We passed an occupied site (the best on the lake) on a point just up from the river and quickly made our way to a tiny island to the north. There we strung up a dining tarp, brewed a cup of tea and huddled inside the tent. But as we prepared ourselves for a soggy night, the clouds suddenly dispersed and a colorful rainbow arched over the distant hills.

The next day Brian and I paddled down the length of Black Lake, taking the rocky 1,000-yard (914 m) portage to the lower marsh on the Black River and then a 370-yard (337 m) portage (marked along the right bank) connecting the lower marsh with the upper marsh. From the upper marsh, there's a rise, to the left, of 250 yards (228 m) around the old logging dam and present control dam on Wren Lake. Cottages decorated the shorelines once again as we headed southeast along Wren, under the Highway 35 bridge. We then continued directly north to Raven Lake via a short carry of 50 yards (46 m), to the right, around the control dam. Brian still teases me about falling in the drink as we pushed off from one of the floating square timbers chained to the dam, so be careful if using the same technique to push off from shore.

Before heading back to the parking lot by the highway via Five Mile Bay to the west, Brian and I decided to paddle to the south, down a narrow channel to the legendary Raven's Cliff. Natives once traveled to this cliff, climbed to its summit and tossed tobacco into the waters below to appease the spirits. Ravens (in Native mythology, guardians over the spirit world) still nest on the windswept cliff, but local Natives haven't thrown tobacco over the rocky height for years.

The most memorable experience during the two days we spent exploring the Black Lake Loop was our dip at Raven's Cliff. After hours of paddling and portaging, Brian and I agreed we needed a bath before we returned to civilization. So we pulled the canoe up on a campsite located directly across from the cliff. The plan was to swim across the channel from the campsite to the base of the cliff, sunbathe on the rocks and swim back to the site. Both Brian and I had forgotten to pack swimming trunks, but the area seemed quite secluded — at least that's what we thought! Brian packed his towel, hairbrush and pants into a garbage bag and blew a puff of air into it before tying it shut. "You've got to be kidding," I joked. "You expect everything to keep dry in that flimsy plastic bag while swimming across?" He smirked and replied, "You're no longer the only experienced outdoorsman on our trips, you know."

We both stripped and quickly waded into the cool water, Brian with his plastic garbage bag and me still badgering him about his new flotation device. It took nearly ten minutes to dog-paddle across the channel to the opposite shore, and by then we literally had to drag our naked bodies up onto the rocks.

While we gasped for air, our secluded swimming hole became a local attraction. As we sat at the base of Raven's Cliff, exhausted from the swim, a motorboat filled with four young women rounded the bend and headed for the shore we had just beached ourselves on. Brian opened his airtight garbage bag, pulled on his perfectly dry pants and wrapped his towel around his shoulders, while I sat there naked as a button. The women soon spotted me and gave a polite wave. They then turned the boat around and sped off, laughing hysterically.

We ended our swim and paddled west across Raven Lake to the parking lot on Highway 35, then hiked back to Shoe Lake to retrieve our vehicle, and completed the Black Lake adventure. During those two days, we had canoed over half a dozen pocket lakes, dragged our boat across a dry river bed, portaged through bug-infested trails, and even "exposed" ourselves to the elements, but boy did we have fun. I think next time, however, I'll pack a swimsuit.

## BLACK LAKE LOOP

**TIME** 2–3 days

**DIFFICULTY** Good physical health and a high level of canoe tripping experience are needed.

**NUMBER OF PORTAGES** 11

**LONGEST PORTAGE** 1,600 yards (1,463 m)

**FEE** The route is situated in the Leslie M. Frost Centre, where no fees are required.

**ALTERNATIVE ACCESS** Wren Lake access point, located on the northeast side of the Highway 35 bridge.

**ALTERNATIVE ROUTE** An easier route may be to simply paddle/ portage in and out of Black Lake by way of the Wren Lake access point.

**FISH SPECIES** Blue Chalk and Red Chalk Lakes offer fair fishing for speckle trout. Blue Chalk also has a small population of lake trout and Red Chalk has decent-sized bass. Carcass and Pairo Lake have bass;

Black Lake and Wren Lake are stocked with splake and both have good bass fishing. Raven Lake has fair lake trout fishing and good bass fishing.

**KAYAK FRIENDLY** No

**OUTFITTERS** None

**FOR MORE INFORMATION**
LESLIE M. FROST CENTRE
R.R. 2
Minden, Ontario
K0M 2K0
705-766-2451

MINISTRY OF NATURAL RESOURCES
Minden District Office
Minden, Ontario
K0M 2K0
705-286-1521

**MAPS** Chrismar Mapping Co. has produced an excellent map detailing the interior canoe routes of the Leslie M. Frost Centre.

**TOPOGRAPHIC MAP** 31 E/2

# Rockaway and Dividing Lakes

**GIANT WHITE PINES ARE AMONG THE SIGHTS** you can look forward to if you take a canoe trip to the western border of Algonquin Provincial Park. A word of caution, though: You must be an experienced tripper and physically fit to tackle this rugged but rewarding two-day route.

The adventure can begin at one of two public access points: Kawagama Lake or Livingstone Lake (Algonquin's access point no. 14). If heavy winds are forecast, choose the Livingstone Lake access, but I prefer to head out from Kawagama (Hollow Lake).

To reach both access points, drive along Highway 36 to Dorset. Just north of the town, turn right onto Kawagama Road. If you choose to drive to Livingstone Lake, follow the road for almost half a mile (0.7 km) to the second junction, turn right and continue for 15 miles (23.6 km) to the road leading to Livingstone Lake Lodge. Take note that if you are using this point of access during the summer months, you must first get a park permit at the general store before turning onto Kawagama Lake Road. Also, make sure not to leave your vehicle at the lodge (the management will have it towed). Park to the right of the road as it bends to the left, away from the lake. A quick paddle down Livingstone Lake, a 350-yard (320 m) portage to the right of a government dam, then another quick paddle down Bear Lake, and you will be on your way to Algonquin's western border.

If you choose to start off on Kawagama Lake, follow Kawagama Road (keeping to the right on Road 8) to its end. A parking lot and boat ramp are available. Paddle across the large lake by making your way between Big Trout and Bear Islands, then keep to the right of Dennison Island and head toward the channel into Bear Lake, located to the northeast.

Be forewarned; it can be a rough crossing if the winds build up. On one trip, some friends and I had to wait until nightfall before the winds subsided. Only then could we proceed across Kawagama. We drifted through darkness, with only the odd haze of northern lights to brighten the sky, and followed the shoreline by listening to the water sucking and gurgling under the banks. My companions became a little uneasy when I told them the tale of Kawagama's ghostly light as we made our way past Dennison Island. Legend has it that if you see a bright light moving across the lake during the night, a member of your party will die before morning. During our midnight crossing, we were lucky enough not to catch a glimpse of such a light. However, the ghost story made us paddle to Bear Lake and up the narrow channel to Kimball Lake in record time.

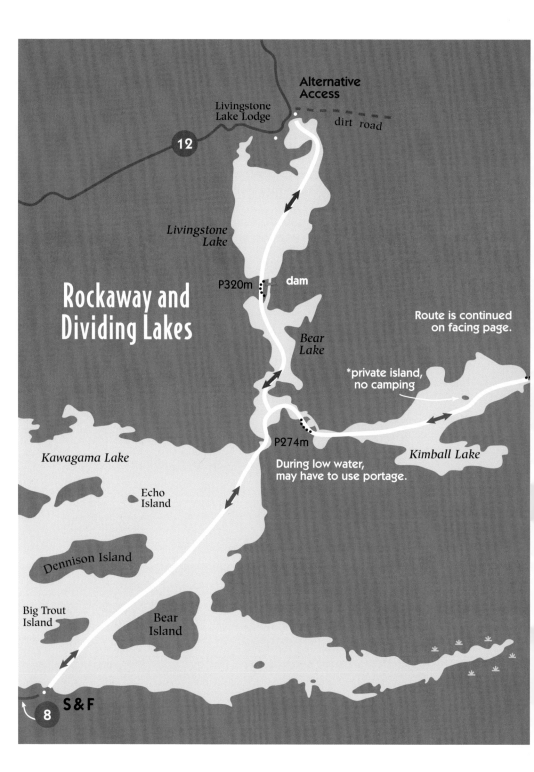

Alternative
Access

Livingstone
Lake Lodge

dirt road

12

Livingstone
Lake

# Rockaway and
Dividing Lakes

P320m  dam

Bear
Lake

Route is continued
on facing page.

*private island,
no camping

Kawagama Lake

P274m

During low water,
may have to use portage.

Kimball Lake

Echo
Island

Dennison Island

Big Trout
Island

Bear
Island

8  S & F

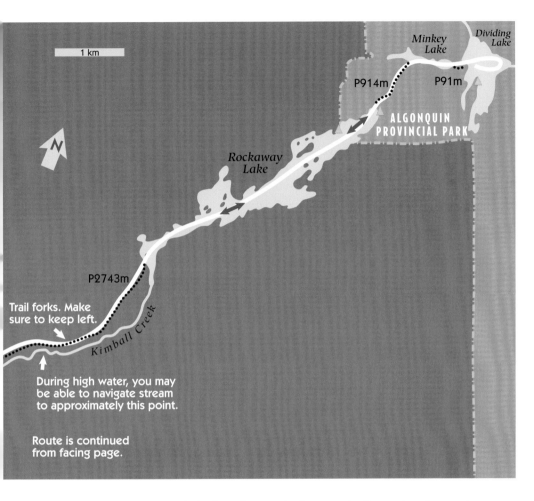

Minkey Lake

Dividing Lake

1 km

P914m

P91m

ALGONQUIN
PROVINCIAL PARK

Rockaway
Lake

P2743m

**Trail forks. Make
sure to keep left.**

Kimball Creek

**During high water, you may
be able to navigate stream
to approximately this point.**

**Route is continued
from facing page.**

My canoe partner and I had not been as lucky on a similar outing the previous year. Scott, an old high school chum, had asked me a month before to guide him and his friends from work, Art and Peter, on a canoe trip to the forest reserve bordering Algonquin Park. On Friday night they arrived at my apartment in Peterborough, only to find me down with a cold.

Early Saturday morning I convinced myself that the previous night's dose of extra-strength Neo Citran had miraculously cured my ailment and we left Peterborough before 6 A.M. The trip appeared to be cursed from the moment we left. We chose to take the Livingstone Lake access point, and due to a late start we didn't dip our paddles until well after 10 A.M. Once on the lake, we made our way along the eastern channel to Kimball Lake, then across the entire length of Kimball to the start of the longest portage. The 3,000-yard (2,743 m) path, nicknamed the Golden Staircase by the locals, works its way through a wet, bug-

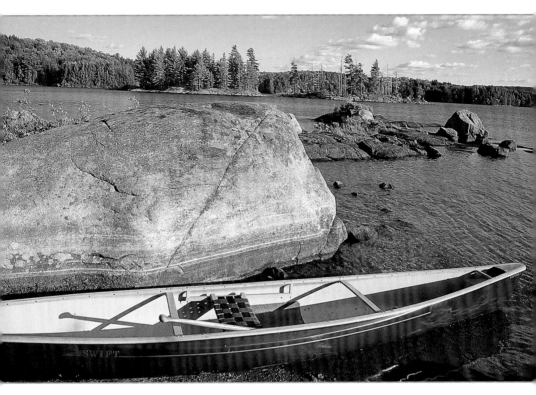

*Above: The Rockaway and Dividing Lake canoe route connects to the western border of Algonquin Provincial Park and an endless chain of lakes and rivers to explore. Facing page: Here's a reason to tackle the dreaded "Golden Staircase" portage: camping among Rockaway Lake's magnificent old-growth white pine.*

infested lowland, then veers north up a steep grade alongside a cascading falls, ending at Rockaway Lake.

Two problems arose while we tackled the Golden Staircase. First, Art and Peter had never really battled pack and canoe for such a great distance, and Art repeatedly made it apparent that he was not having a good time. Second, it quickly became obvious to the guiding party, yours truly, that portaging a total of 6.25 miles (10 km) over rugged terrain with a chest cold, runny nose and laryngitis was not what the doctor ordered. The one thing that pushed me on was the comforting realization that I'd done all this before, and even with a hacking cough draining my energy, I knew I would get through it again. Scott, Art and Peter simply didn't realize that subjecting oneself to such an exhausting, uncomfortable ordeal is part of the canoe-tripping experience.

It was just after 6 P.M. by the time we completed the portage and paddled to the end of Rockaway Lake to make camp on the border of the forest reserve, home of giant, age-old white pine. In minutes I erected my tent, unrolled my sleeping bag and boiled chicken noodle soup. After a generous amount of Tylenol and a cup of hot tea, I went straight to bed.

*If water levels are high and beaver activity is low, there is a small creek you can navigate to help shorten the 3,000-yard (2,743 m) portage into Rockaway Lake.*

A chilling frost visited camp that night, freezing the water bottles and leaving me with a fever. By morning my cold was so bad that I feared for my long-term health. While Scott, Art and Peter took the day to paddle into Dividing Lake to fish for speckled trout, I spent the day in camp fighting my fever. I transformed my tent into a sweat hut. By mid-afternoon, after many prayers and a couple of hours spent leaning over steaming rocks, my fever began to break. With a clear head and nose, I decided to walk back into the bush from the campsite to visit the giant pines on the portage between Minkey and Dividing Lake.

There they stood, among the even more impressive hemlock and yellow birch, lonely monarchs of the forest. How these few giant pines hid from the loggers of the past I have no idea. The rugged terrain that we struggled across to reach the trees could have been what saved them. Out of all Southern Ontario's forests, only this small stand survives. Two hundred years of age, 165 feet (50 m) in height, the trees are so broad at their trunks that three people cannot reach around them. As I viewed the scant remains of Ontario's primeval wilderness, my fever mysteriously vanished.

We made it back safely to the Livingstone Lake access (via the same route), and I ended up pushing penicillin for a week, cursing myself for not having been smart enough to cancel the canoe trip when I had the chance. But I must admit that fighting that fever en route, as insane as it might have been, made me feel confident about battling the next trip to Haliburton's "Staircase to the Giants."

# ROCKAWAY AND DIVIDING LAKES

**TIME** 2–3 days

**DIFFICULTY** Good physical health and a high level of canoe tripping experience is needed.

**NUMBER OF PORTAGES** 4 (all of which must be doubled back on)

**LONGEST PORTAGE** 3,000 yards (2,743 m) (Golden Staircase)

**FEE** Most of the route is situated on Crown land, and no fee is required for Canadian citizens. The route north of Rockaway Lake, however, is part of Algonquin Provincial Park, and a permit needs to be purchased for this portion.

**ALTERNATIVE ACCESS** Livingstone Lake access, reached by taking the second junction off Kawagama Lake Road (almost half a mile [0.7 km] from the Highway 35 turn-off) and then turning right and continuing for 14.5 miles (23.6 km) to the road leading to Livingstone Lake Lodge.

**ALTERNATIVE ROUTE** To avoid paddling across the expanse of Kawagama Lake, put in at the Livingstone Lake access point and paddle/portage Livingstone Lake and Bear Lake.

**FISH SPECIES** Kawagama, Livingstone, Bear, Kimball and Rockaway have fair to good fishing for lake trout and bass. Dividing Lake offers excellent fishing for speckle (brook) trout.

**KAYAK FRIENDLY** No

**OUTFITTERS**
ALGONQUIN OUTFITTERS
R.R. 1
Dwight, Ontario
P0A 1H0
705-635-2243
www.algonquinoutfitters.com

**FOR MORE INFORMATION**
ALGONQUIN PROVINCIAL PARK
Ministry of Natural Resources
Box 219
Whitney, Ontario
K0J 2M0
705-633-5572
reservations 1-888-668-7275

**TOPOGRAPHIC MAPS**
31 E/7 & 31 E/8

# Poker Lake Loop

**THE MINISTRY OF NATURAL RESOURCES** (MNR) suggests that canoeists initiate their two-day trip on the Poker Lake Loop from Cinder Lake, north of Highway 118. I first canoed the loop during the summer of 1990, and I followed these directions and launched my canoe from Cinder Lake, but by the end of the weekend my opinion on the suggested access point differed from the Ministry's.

While traveling the chain of lakes, I decided to camp on Bentshoe Lake, halfway along the loop. Here I made an unpleasant discovery: Every site had been previously occupied by groups of "party animals." The revellers had reached Bentshoe by simply carrying their boomboxes and coolers of beer down from the highway, which was just 110 yards (100 m) away. Needless to say, the situation did not make me a happy camper.

It took a year before I was ready to give the Poker Lake route a second chance. This time, I chose a weekend in late autumn when the only wildlife in the area was adorned with fur or feathers. And instead of driving to Cinder Lake, I simply drove 13 miles (20 km) from the junction of Highways 118 and 35 and parked my vehicle in the designated parking area on the south side of the highway. A 110-yard (100 m) portage took me to Bentshoe Lake, where I began a perfect trip through the Poker Lake Loop. (Be careful while crossing the highway from the parking lot to the portage leading down to Bentshoe Lake.)

Traveling clockwise, one must paddle the length of Bentshoe to the northern bay. A 350-yard (325 m) portage, the longest on the route, takes you to scenic Poker Lake. Follow the north shore until you find the 55 yard (50 m) portage into a small, weedy pond (Ooze Lake). At times, especially in low water, trying to navigate through this weedy, stump-infested body of water is next to impossible. It's best to keep to the right and follow a network of muskrat paths. The 80-yard (75 m) portage into Quirt Lake from the north end of the pond may also have to be extended to avoid getting caught in swamp ooze.

Quirt Lake is divided in half, with a small channel joining the south and north ends. Just before the narrow passage there is a nice lunch spot high up on a rock outcrop to the right. The site is secluded and high enough to offer a breeze as bug repellent. After a well-deserved break, paddle to the far western bay of Quirt Lake, where the last portage of the day (80 yards [75 m]) can be found marked at the northern tip of the swampy basin.

Once you finish the portage and begin to paddle across Cinder Lake, you will realize why I would much rather end the day than start it from this isolated lake. A large island and other smaller islands sprinkled across the lake make

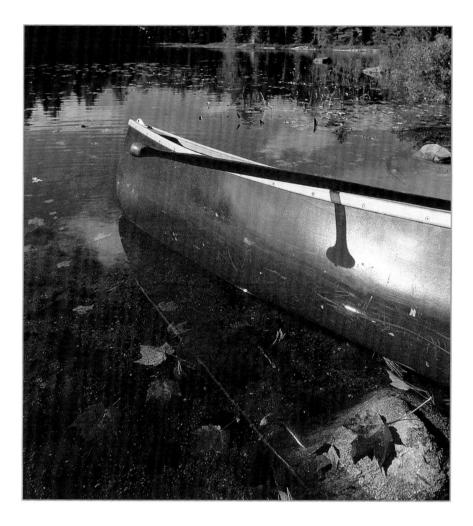

excellent campsites. My favorite place to spend the night is on the southern tip of the main island, halfway across Cinder. At this point the island appears to split the lake in two.

During my stay here, I watched a family of otters munch on crayfish on a small rock outcrop directly across from camp. After the feast they washed their paws and faces, slid into the water and bobbed up and down, watching me eat my dinner of freeze-dried stew.

If time permits, paddle to Cinder's northwest end and search for the hull of a sunken logging boat resting on some rocks, a small piece of evidence of Haliburton's logging days.

The trip begins the next day by taking the 190-yard (175 m) portage southeast of the previously mentioned campsite, out of Cinder Lake and into another small pond. This section can be grueling in low water, and the last time I used the trail it was overgrown with thick patches of raspberry bushes. Unfortunately I was wearing shorts and a T-shirt that day — not the best apparel for bushwhacking.

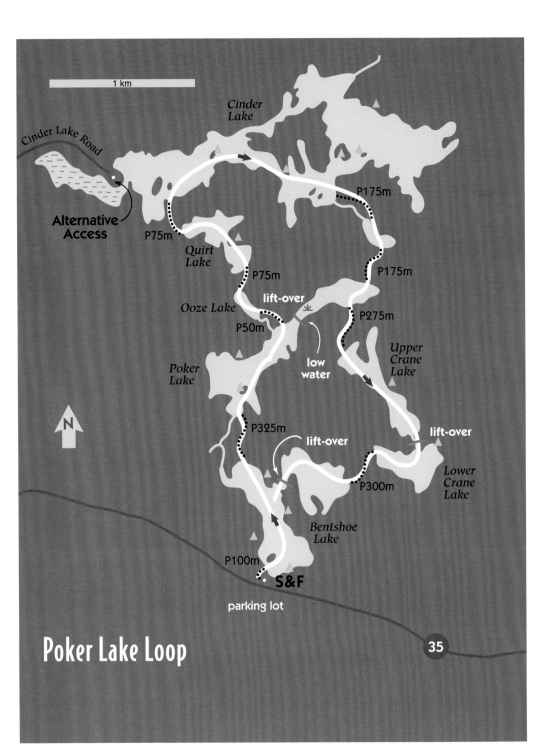

1 km

Cinder
Lake

Cinder Lake Road

P175m

**Alternative Access**

P75m

*Quirt Lake*

P75m

*Ooze Lake*

**lift-over**

P175m

P50m

P275m

*Upper Crane Lake*

**low water**

*Poker Lake*

P325m

**lift-over**

**lift-over**

P300m

*Lower Crane Lake*

N

*Bentshoe Lake*

P100m

**S&F**

parking lot

**Poker Lake Loop**

35

The next portage, also 190 yards (175 m), is at the south end of the shallow pond, and if memory serves me well, the time I traveled the route in midsummer I sank up to my knees in loon scat, trying to pull my canoe to the beginning of the poorly marked path. This muddy portage takes you to the eastern arm of Poker Lake, where you paddle directly across to reach yet another portage, this one being 110 yards (100 m) longer than the previous ones.

The path into Upper Crane Lake is relatively easy, as is the 330-yard (300 m) portage out of Lower Crane and into the eastern bay of the familiar Bentshoe Lake, located at the lake's western tip. Where Upper and Lower Crane join, however, can be quite an arduous passage if water levels are low. To make it through the junction, I once had to tie my bowline to my waist and jump from one floating bog mat to the other. If I hadn't spotted the curious family of otters furtively trailing behind me, I would have once again given second thought to returning to the Poker Lake canoe route. Thanks to the inquisitive otter family, as well as the scenic splendor of Cinder Lake, I have gone back many times to this enjoyable two-day loop on the western border of Haliburton County.

## POKER LAKE LOOP

**TIME** 2 days

**DIFFICULTY** A moderate level of canoe tripping experience is needed.

**NUMBER OF PORTAGES** 9

**LONGEST PORTAGE** 330 yards (300 m)

**FEE** The Poker Lake Loop is situated on Crown land, and no fee is needed for Canadian citizens.

**ALTERNATIVE ACCESS** Cinder Lake can be accessed by using Cinder Lake Road, north of Highway 118. However, it is not recommended as it is no longer maintained.

**ALTERNATIVE ROUTE** Big East Lake, a much easier route, can be accessed directly across from the Poker Lake Loop.

**FISH SPECIES** Poker, Bentshoe and Cinder Lakes provide good bass fishing. Upper and Lower Crane have been stocked with splake.

**KAYAK FRIENDLY** No

**OUTFITTERS** None

**FOR MORE INFORMATION** MINISTRY OF NATURAL RESOURCES Minden District Office Minden, Ontario K0M 2K0 705-286-1521

**MAPS** Chrismar Mapping Co. has produced an excellent map detailing the Poker Lake canoe route.

**TOPOGRAPHIC MAP** 31 E/2

# Big East Lake

**FOR TEN YEARS NOW I'VE WORKED** as a part-time Environmental Issues instructor at Sir Sandford Fleming College in Lindsay, Ontario. The course mostly deals with human overpopulation, pollution, resource extraction, the lack of biodiversity, and even the fallacy of conservation. Basically it's a general outlook on our high-handed, superior views toward nature, and quite honestly the job gets darn depressing at times.

A few years back — after weeks of lecturing on toxic spills, clear cutting, the extinction of species — I had to give my students some encouragement, a little dash of hope. So I handed out an assignment where they had to research a "good news" case study, something that was a positive approach toward caring for our environment. A week later they gathered into the lecture hall, handed me their papers, and firmly stated that it was the most difficult assignment I had ever given them. Not for the marking scheme itself — I'm one of the less demanding professors at the college — but the fact that each student found nothing other than a handful of band-aid solutions.

Imagine my dilemma. I had to mark all these daunting case studies and, for the students' sake, still remain optimistic. Realizing that the best place to gain a positive outlook toward nature was nature itself, I packed up my canoe gear immediately after class and headed north to Haliburton's Big East Lake. The lake, situated directly across from the more popular Poker Lake Loop, is a perfect quick fix for canoeists (or depressed environmental issues instructors looking to re-energize themselves).

It was a good two-hour drive to the parking area on the south side of Highway 118, 12.5 miles (20 km) west of Highway 35, and another 20 minutes to double-carry my canoe and pack down the 220-yard (200 m) trail to the launch site. By the time I paddled to the far southwest end of the lake to make camp on a large island, carpeted with a good stand of pine and white birch, I just had enough light to erect my tent and gather a bundle of firewood.

After a quick dinner, I brewed up a large pot of tea, and by the dime light of the campfire, I marked papers well into the night.

I was a little late for my nine o'clock class the next day. But when I finally wandered into the lecture hall to meet my students, offering excuses for my tardiness and the pungent smell of smoke coming off my clothes, the news that I had their papers already marked and that each student received a passing grade helped erase any ill feelings. With an upbeat attitude, I continued to lecture that day, talking about the pleasures of wild places and the willingness most of us

*Bailey — the runt of the litter but a perfect canoe dog.*

have to protect the familiar, once we become familiar with it. And to this day I make an annual pilgrimage back to Big East Lake, not with students' assignments but rather with the students themselves. In fact, an overnight canoe trip to Big East Lake has become a prerequisite for my course. It's a tad more work than simply marking essays but I think it's a far more effective teaching tool.

## BIG EAST LAKE

**DIFFICULTY** Novice

**PORTAGES** One (the trail leading down to the canoe launch)

**LONGEST PORTAGE** 220 yards (200 m)

**FEE** Big East Lake is situated on Crown land, and no fee is required for Canadian citizens.

**ALTERNATIVE ACCESS** No

**ALTERNATIVE ROUTE** The Poker Lake Loop is a two-day loop accessed directly across from the Big East parking lot and makes an excellent side trip).

**KAYAK FRIENDLY** Yes

**FISH SPECIES** Big East Lake has good bass fishing and is stocked with splake.

**OUTFITTERS** None

**FOR MORE INFORMATION**
MINISTRY OF NATURAL RESOURCES
Minden District Office
Box 820
Minden, Ontario
K0M 2K0
705-286-1521

**MAPS** A good reference is the *Poker Lake Adventure Map*, produced by Chrismar Mapping Service.

**TOPOGRAPHICAL MAP**
Haliburton 31 E/2

## Burnt River System

Along the fringe of the Kawartha and Haliburton regions, one can choose from two routes, both part of the Burnt River system. The fast-flowing Irondale River gushes down from the town of Gooderham, while the slow-moving, snakelike Drag River flows from Lake Canning; both join the Burnt northeast of Kinmount.

# Irondale-Burnt Rivers

**IF I HAD TO CHOOSE** between the two river routes, I would have to say that I'd much rather spend the weekend traveling the Irondale and Burnt River system. Two short but challenging days will take you from Gooderham to Kinmount. To reach Gooderham, drive east on Highway 503 from Kinmount, where a second (pick-up) vehicle must first be parked at the town boat launch (just past the grocery store). The starting point is just south of the small hamlet of Gooderham, across the bridge on the left-hand side of the road.

Soon after launching your canoe, you will come to the first of many short portages. This portage (410 yards [375 m]) is located on the right bank. Depending on the water levels and your experience, you may opt to line or run a number of the whitewater sections along the river. Farther downriver, you'll notice the remnants of an old railway line following alongside. In fact, the next portage to your right (645 yards [590 m]) uses the line to avoid a shallow boulder garden and granite gorge.

The railway line was established in 1880 and was called the I.B. & O. Railway. The line may have served the Burnt River area loyally, but it was constantly criticized for being the railway that ran from nowhere to nowhere. Because it continued to lose money, it was soon nicknamed the "I.O.U." line. The I.B. & O. was initially constructed in response to the iron-mining rush of 1878–86, and was later extended from the mining town of Furnace Falls to Gooderham under the direction of two Americans, Henry Howland and Charles Pusey. At one time the "I.O.U." Railway had to be granted a loan to help it out of debt. The loan was made under the condition that the extension be completed by a certain date. Howland and Pusey knew the deadline would be impossible to meet, so they came up with an ingenious scheme to leap-frog the first train to Gooderham. After laying dozens of ties and a few sections of track, the workers drove the train down the new track, then ripped up the track over which the train had just passed, and used this to continue the line ahead of the train. This may not have been the most appropriate method of laying line, but Gooderham got their first train on schedule and the I.B. & O. got their loan.

*Above: Burnt River's Three Brothers Falls.*
*Below: Late fall portaging along the Irondale River.*

The next five portages are close together and short in length, ranging from 35 yards to 130 yards (32–120 m). Each portage is located to the right of the river, except for the fifth, which can be spotted on the left bank. The Ministry of Natural Resources claims that this section of the river carries brook trout and bass, and that down below Three Brothers Falls an angler can find walleye and muskie. However, I've cast about in the pools and eddies for brook trout with no luck.

The next portage (380 yards [350 m]), located to the right, makes its way around a whitewater section in the river that the locals call the Devil's Gap. After the Devil's Gap, follow along one more portage (175 yards [160 m]), marked to the

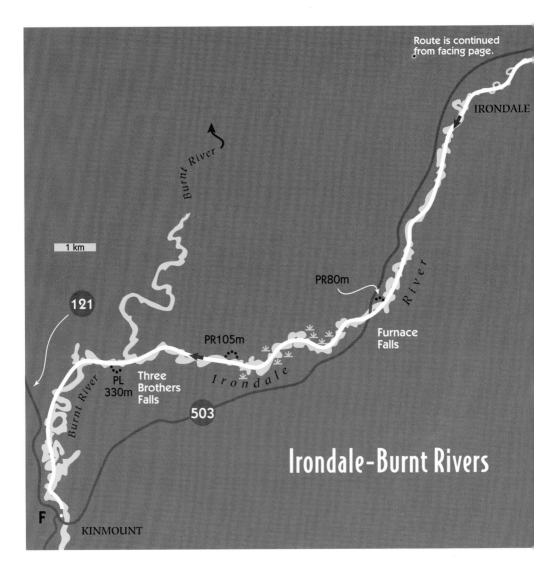

Route is continued from facing page.

IRONDALE

*Burnt River*

1 km

*River*

PR80m

121

*River*

PR105m

Furnace Falls

Three Brothers Falls

*Burnt River*

*Irondale*

PL 330m

503

**Irondale-Burnt Rivers**

F

KINMOUNT

right. At the end of the trail, you will find a designated campsite on the left bank. You can pitch your tent here, making the first day short but adventurous. Due to the fact that almost all the land along the Irondale is privately owned, this is the only designated site on the route to Kinmount. To ensure the future of this priceless canoe route, please show the utmost courtesy when dealing with landowners along the river. If you are caught in a tight spot (campsites on the entire river are on a first come, first served basis), make sure to ask permission from the landowner before using areas other than those posted with signs.

One evening I was entertained by a mink at this scenic campsite. Apparently not bothered by my presence, the slinky mammal stood on the river bank only a few feet away, watching for fish. Of course, the moment I reached for my camera the mink slithered into the water, never to be seen again.

On day two, you have a longer distance to cover, so make sure you are on the river early. This part of the Irondale is no different than the others: You have only to paddle around the next bend before being forced to portage around a section of water that gouges through the hard gneiss and comes to rest in a quiet pool. Look for the 230-yard (210 m) portage on the left bank.

From the pool you'll catch a glimpse of Contau Lake Road, then the river curves to the right, meanders under a small bridge and works its way through a changing landscape. The pine that were rooted in granite are now replaced by an entanglement of maple, ash and dogwood. At this point the river begins to slow its momentum over the land. Only three short portages lie in wait between Contau Lake Road and Furnace Falls, east of Highway 503. The first two are to the right of a bend in the river and measure 110 yards (100 m). The third portage,

*Almost continuous rapids along the upper stretch of the Irondale River make this route a haven for whitewater fanatics.*

only 22 yards (20 m), is soon to follow; it is located on the left bank where the old railway line used to cross the river.

Once past the town of Irondale, a 5.5-mile (9 km) stretch of quiet, portage-free water is to be enjoyed. The roar of the river becomes a distant murmur and is replaced by the delightful sound of small warblers singing in the brush. Local legend has it that the stillness in the river comes from a curse by ghosts. Certain people believe that the whole area has been plagued with bad luck since Michael Dean first surveyed it in the mid-1800s. While performing his survey, Dean noticed an extraordinary fluctuation in his compass needle, which led him to discover the presence of iron ore. It wasn't long before the iron rush was on and the bad happenings began. Snowdown Iron was the first company to mine the area, in 1874, and was vexed by financial difficulties from start to finish. It wasn't until 1876 that several hundred tons of ore were finally cadged to the new railway in Kinmount and then shipped to Cleveland. But the company's fortune was sunk before the shipment could reach its port.

The hamlet of Furnace Falls began to show signs of progress, including the construction of a mine smelter-sawmill complex, but was wiped off the map by a raging forest fire in the dry summer of 1887.

Just before you reach Highway 503, an 88-yard (80 m) portage to your right makes its way around the cascading Furnace Falls and through a roadside park. Directly across from the park is the gravesite of the ghost town's giant blast furnace that gives the falls its name.

Downriver the current flows under Highway 503 and keeps a steady moderate pace, winding through the landscape like a serpent, altered only by Jacob's

Ladder (another set of rapids). The rapids can be avoided by a 115-yard (105 m) portage to the right.

Almost 2 miles (3 km) from Jacob's Ladder, the Irondale merges with the Burnt–Drag River system from the north. From here on in you're on the Burnt River. Shortly after, you arrive at one of the most splendid sights of the Burnt River route — Three Brothers Falls. The 360-yard (330 m) portage along the left bank, which again follows the old railway line, offers an excellent view of each "brother," the last being the most dramatic.

A little more than an hour of paddling will get you to the lift-out point at the town of Kinmount. Along the way, you will pass through a maze of marshy inlets where giant muskie hunt for unsuspecting goslings, and snapping turtles bathe in swamp muck. To avoid getting lost along this section, keep to your right. An added day can be spent canoeing from Kinmount. Follow the river (described in the Drag–Burnt River route) downstream to Fenelon Falls.

## IRONDALE–BURNT RIVERS

**TIME** 1–2 days

**DIFFICULTY** A moderate level of canoe tripping skills and some experience paddling whitewater is needed.

**NUMBER OF PORTAGES** 16

**LONGEST PORTAGE** 645 yards (590 m) (not all portages are necessary)

**FEE** The Irondale–Burnt River route is situated, for the most part, on Crown land and no fee is needed for Canadian citizens.

**ALTERNATIVE ACCESS** Furnace Falls public picnic site, east side of Highway 503.

**ALTERNATIVE ROUTE** The trip can be shortened to a one-day outing by paddling from Gooderham to Irondale or from Furnace Falls to Kinmount.

**FISH SPECIES** The upper Irondale has small brook trout. Walleye and muskellunge can also be caught below Three Brothers Falls, and bass can be caught throughout.

**KAYAK FRIENDLY** No

**OUTFITTERS**
BOAT WORKS
Highway 35
Minden, Ontario
K0M 2K0
705-286-1492

**FOR MORE INFORMATION**
MINISTRY OF NATURAL RESOURCES
Minden District Office
Minden, Ontario
K0M 2K0
705-286-1521

**TOPOGRAPHIC MAPS**
31 D/10, 31 D/15 & 31 D/16

# Drag–Burnt Rivers

**LIKE THE IRONDALE,** the Drag River is home to the occasional bridge, cabin and ghost town. Its waters are filtered by dense stands of second-growth mixed forest. The land surrounding the Burnt River system may not be absolutely wild, but the river remains pristine, and to a river runner that's all that matters at times. If you're a less adventurous canoeist, the Drag–Burnt River route will be more to your liking. Unlike the Irondale, the Drag and upper Burnt have few rapids and can usually be run right into midsummer.

I know canoeists who head out from the Haliburton town docks, paddling through Head, Grass, Kashagawigamog and Canning Lakes, but I prefer a more direct route and usually get on to the Drag River at the Canning Lake Dam. By starting out from the dam, you can cut 12 miles (half a day's paddle) from a 50-mile route (about 20 of 80 km). It will then only take two days to canoe the 38 miles (60 km) to either Fenelon Falls or Balsam Lake Provincial Park, where your second vehicle should be waiting.

To reach the dam, take Highway 121 through the town of Kinmount and make a right onto Route No. 1, heading toward the hamlet of Gelert. North of Gelert, the road crosses the Drag River. Instead of going over the bridge, turn left toward Canning Lake Dam, where a parking area is available on the same side of the river.

To put in, cross over the dam and take the 110-yard (100 m) portage down to the river. Just south of the dam, you paddle under the bridge. You must either navigate the rapids or line your canoe within the bounds of the riverbed. Don't worry, this is not difficult.

The third and fourth portages (188 yards and 330 yards [172 m, 300 m], respectively), both located to the left, can be lined or walked through, depending on water levels. Just under the third bridge, near the town of Gelert, you will come across yet another portage (426 yards [390 m]), which works its way around a set of rapids along the right bank.

The sleepy town of Gelert was once a thriving community. It became a boomtown between 1880 and 1890 with the coming of the railway and settlers who chopped back the forest to farm the area's arable soil. After 1900, the Gelert railway station closed and farming declined.

Past the town of Gelert, the Drag River becomes the Burnt River and snakes along, portage free, until it meets up with the Irondale River just before Three Brothers Falls. This meandering section of the river is a haven for river otters. These creatures have often played alongside my canoe. Broadleaf foliage grows

*Low water levels on the upper reaches of the Burnt River can make for difficult paddling at times.*

in thick patches along the sand bars and overhanging banks. The lower brush furnishes ideal cover for yellow warblers and redstarts, and the timbered slopes provide shelter for woodpeckers, brown creepers and nuthatches.

If you're trying to shorten your days on the water and plan not to paddle all the way to Cameron Lake, there is a designated campsite marked halfway between the town of Gelert and Three Brothers Falls. The public land, dubbed "Dahl Forest," was donated to the province by Peter Dahl, a local cottage owner and avid canoeist who has been known to invite the odd canoe party in for a cup of coffee during dreary days in early spring.

Downstream from the piece of Crown land, the waters of the Burnt and Irondale rivers converge. Shortly after, a 360-yard (330 m) portage awaits you to the left of the scenic Three Brothers Falls. Make sure to use the well-worn path, for the drop past the portage is no place to be, experienced or not. A few years ago a United States marine attempted to paddle over the Three Brothers in a Grumman canoe. Somehow he made it over the first two sets of falls, but his aluminum canoe was sucked into the water below the last set of falls. The river finally spat out the wreckage later in the day. Luckily the marine was thrown from the canoe on the way over and miraculously escaped the mad pool without a scratch. He camped below the falls with his aluminum scrap heap until help eventually arrived.

Canning Lake

Portage located across dam.
PL 100m

to Haliburton

Burnt River

# Drag–Burnt Rivers

**S**

Canning Lake Dam

PL172m

Drag River

PL 300m

N

GELERT

PL390m

121

1

Burnt River

Irondale River

Three Brothers Falls

503

PL 330m

**Alternative Access**

KINMOUNT

PR235m

Old Kinmount Dam

PR40m

High Falls

PR375m

3 km

503

PR60m

Route is continued at top of facing page.

Route is continued from bottom of facing page.

649

503

PL60m

PR430m

PR240m

PR40m

*Four
Mile
Lake*

35

*Corben Creek*

*Burnt River*

48

Canoeists
can choose
between 2
routes to
finish.

*North Bay*

F

Indian
Point

**BALSAM LAKE
PROVINCIAL
PARK**

121

*Rosedale*

*River*

FENELON
FALLS

*Grand
Island*

*Balsam
Lake*

*Cameron
Lake*

F

After the falls, the river once again calms down, although you will encounter the occasional boiling pulse on the surface, reminding you of the current below. Once you have navigated through the swampland that comes next, you will arrive at the town of Kinmount. You can end a perfect day by putting out here. However, if you choose to continue, you will find that the river is quite beautiful downstream.

At Kinmount the river flows under a modern concrete-and-metal bridge. Almost immediately after this bridge, you are forced to portage around the historic Kinmount Dam. The 257-yard (235 m) trail is located to the right and makes its way around the ruins of an old mill. The dam was built in 1858 by John Hunter. By 1859, Hunter operated a mill on the east side of the dam, as well as a grist mill on the downstream side of the sawmill. In addition to the two mills, Hunter owned a store, hotel, tavern and stables. In fact, John Hunter was such an ambitious man that he is known by many locals as the founder of Kinmount.

In 1874, W.H. Greene, a lumberman from Fenelon Falls, erected a mill on the site of the present Austin Mill (built in 1909). To keep the mill working all season, at least 12,000 logs were needed. Since these logs were stored in the river, the waterway was often filled with logs from the dam back to Three Brothers Falls.

The lumber barons built dams all along the Burnt River system to maximize water levels and keep a steady flow for as long as possible. Before the railway came to the area, the lumbermen relied on the river to transport their logs. The Burnt carried millions of logs during the boom years. At times the timber slide at Kinmount dam saw 200,000 logs per season. A logbook entry made in May 1880 indicated that 80,000 logs went through in only four days.

Downstream from the dam you will paddle through what I refer to as a historic garbage dump. Here, the river's banks are cluttered with old cars, trucks and machinery from years gone by. Soon after the dump you will come to a short set of rapids that can be avoided by a 44-yard (40 m) portage to the right. A mile or so later, another portage is necessary. This 410-yard (375 m) path, which is also located to the right, works its way around a magnificent set of falls followed by a short, twisted set of rapids. It's best to portage around the entire length. I once attempted the rapids with Gertrude, and she now bears patches on her bow.

From the falls, paddle another mile (1.5 km), until the river makes a sharp bend southward. To the right a sharp sandy cliff, home to swallows and kingfishers, cuts into a shadowed pool, and to the left a designated campsite can be found on top of a grassy outcrop. The site itself is not the best and is therefore rarely used by canoeists. However, I once spent a memorable morning there, sipping coffee and watching a Cooper's hawk preying upon the cliff swallows for breakfast.

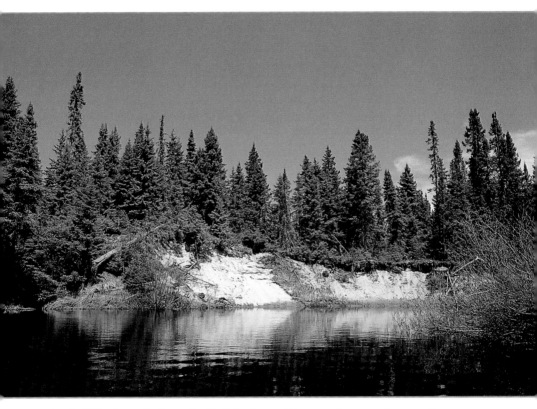

*Sand cliffs along the lower half of the Burnt River are home to dozens of swallows and kingfishers.*

There are three other campsites to choose from. The first comes immediately after the site just mentioned. The other two are between 3.5 to 5 miles (6–8 km) south. But it may be too late in the day to canoe any farther downstream.

If you plan to paddle to Fenelon Falls or Balsam Lake the next day, you had better be on the river early. But if you prefer, you can end the trip before then, at one of the four road bridges, and enjoy sleeping late.

Not far from your campsite, you will come across the first portage of day two, a 66-yard (60 m) path to the right. The waterway turns calm again until just before the second road bridge, where another 66-yard (60 m) portage is marked to the right. Between the second and third road bridges, three more portages (respectively, 470 yards, 262 yards and 44 yards [430 m, 240 m, 40 m]), all marked along the left bank, force you off the river. After the fourth road bridge, however, you can enjoy the river uninterrupted all the way to the route's end.

Once you arrive at the point where the Burnt River meets the open Rosedale River, travel south along the left channel and cross Cameron Lake if you wish to put out at Fenelon Falls. Or paddle directly west, past the town of Rosedale and across Balsam Lake to Balsam Lake Provincial Park, situated on the western shore of Balsam's north bay.

It may be cheaper to park your vehicle at Fenelon Falls, but I prefer to end on Balsam because of its historical significance. This is the place where in the 1740s the Mississauga helped the Huron chase the Iroquois from their lands and back to the south of the Great Lakes. An Iroquois war party battled the Mississauga at Indian Point on Balsam Lake and were eventually driven upriver to Lake Kashagawigamog, where they fought to the death. (It is said that the bones of the vanquished warriors still wash up on the shores of both lakes.) However, the main battle was fought northwest of Bobcaygeon. It eventually fell back to the Otonabee River, where a thousand warriors died before the Iroquois retreated to New York State. Huronia and the helpless Huron were finally avenged after 100 years of domination by the Iroquois.

## DRAG–BURNT RIVERS

**TIME** 1–2 days

**DIFFICULTY** Novice to intermediate canoe tripping experience needed.

**NUMBER OF PORTAGES** 13

**LONGEST PORTAGE** 470 yards (430 m) (not all portages are necessary)

**FEE** The Drag–Burnt River route is situated, for the most part, on Crown land, and no fee is needed for Canadian citizens.

**ALTERNATIVE ACCESS** Kinmount Public Boat Launch, located on the northeast side of the Highway 121 bridge, just past the local grocery store.

**ALTERNATIVE ROUTE** The trip can be shortened to a short one-day outing by paddling downstream from Kinmount to one of the many side roads crossing the river or paddling upstream from Kinmount to Three Brothers Falls, returning via the same route.

**FISH SPECIES** Walleye and muskellunge can be caught below Three Brothers Falls, bass are found throughout the route, and brown trout have recently been stocked on the lower section of the Burnt River.

**KAYAK FRIENDLY** No

**OUTFITTERS**
BOAT WORKS
Highway 35
Minden, Ontario
K0M 2K0
705-286-1492

**FOR MORE INFORMATION**
MINISTRY OF NATURAL RESOURCES
Minden District Office
Minden, Ontario
K0M 2K0
705-286-1521

**TOPOGRAPHIC MAPS**
31 D/10, 31 D/15 & 31 D/16

# The Kawarthas
## Birthplace of the Modern Canoe

**MORE THAN 10,000 YEARS AGO,** the Kawartha region was bulldozed by four glaciers, each a mile thick. As a result, the area boasts an undulating pattern of lakes and rivers among ridges and hills. Geologists believe this to be one of the most important geological boundaries in Canada — the southern edge of the Canadian Shield, a true paddler's paradise.

In 1615, Samuel de Champlain became the first white man to paddle through the Kawarthas. He was guided by the Huron of Georgian Bay, who were on their way to battle the Iroquois in New York State. Champlain was impressed with this historic aquatic highway, writing in his journal that the area was "fine and of pleasing character."

For 200 years the land that the Mississauga natives called Ka-wa-tha, meaning "bright water and happy lands," became the preferred route of the missionaries and fur traders.

The area was first settled by European immigrants in the early 1800s, and they soon developed a love of paddling the lakes and rivers. Writer Catherine Parr Traill, one of the early settlers, preferred traveling by canoe. She wrote: "I had the honour of being paddled home by Mrs. Peter in a new canoe, just launched, and really the motion was delightful, seated on the bottom of the little bark on a few light hemlock bows, I enjoyed my voyage home exceedingly."

By the 19th century, settlers were obtaining birchbark or dugout canoes from the local Natives so that they could participate in number of annual regattas. Given the demand for watercraft in the area, it is no surprise that the first modern canoe originated in the Kawarthas.

Fed up with portaging a heavy dugout, settler John Stephenson was inspired to build a lighter, more streamlined canoe. In 1858, Stephenson, along with Tom Gordon, manufactured the first plank-and-rib canoe.

There was soon worldwide demand for the Peterborough canoe. Surveyors traveled the West and North with the aid of Peterboroughs. A Lakefield canoe was allegedly the first to be paddled across the English Channel. Even Theodore Roosevelt and Queen Elizabeth paddled cedar-rib canoes built in the Kawarthas. But it was the area where these famous canoe craftsmen obtained their building material that attracted canoeists by the hundreds. In 1907 a tourism brochure advertised this land of "bright water and happy lands" as "the playground of the Continent."

Now, with Crown land and provincial parks preserving some of the best remaining routes in the Kawarthas, there still exist secluded pockets of semi-wild lakes and rivers lying in sweet abandonment, where a canoeist can become lost for the weekend in an ancient paddler's paradise.

# Kawartha Highlands Park

**IN 1988 VINCENT KERRIO,** minister of Natural Resources, stated, "The government believes that the need to preserve a certain amount of 'pure' wilderness is too important to compromise." So, on May 17, without compromise, the number of provincial parks in Ontario was increased from 217 to 270. Among the additional 56 parks, a 4,450-acre (1,800 ha) nature reserve in the hub of the Kawarthas was classified as a natural environment park, and Kawartha Highlands Provincial Park was born.

I canoed the two main bodies of water, Bottle and Sucker Lakes, before the area was classified as a provincial park and after its status changed. Nothing much has been altered, although the sites may be somewhat cleaner; so far the ministry has only acted as a custodian to the newly formed park, picking up garbage from the designated interior campsites. On one trip alone they gathered enough trash to fill a half-ton truck.

To access the park, drive north of Buckhorn along the 507 toward the town of Gooderham. Take the Beaver Lake Road for 2 miles (3 km) to Catchacoma Lake access (located before the bridge to your right). Paddle under the bridge, heading northwest, along the bay of Catchacoma, then follow the east shoreline until you come to the second inlet. Use the 66-yard (60 m) portage to the left of the dam to get into Bottle Creek.

The trip down the wide, slow creek takes a good hour. Clumps of cedars and patches of purple iris grow along the banks, while toward Bottle Lake, 150-year-old hemlock and rare white oak and white ash can be found. The creek finally works its way into a swampy bay on the southern tip of Bottle Lake. Paddle north into Bottle and head to the second bay along the eastern shoreline, where you'll find the steep 200-yard (180 m) portage into Sucker Lake. The portage crosses through an area that was burned over in a major fire in 1913.

Many canoeists use the designated sites on Bottle instead of carrying over into Sucker Lake. The former's sandy beaches and the smallmouth bass that were stocked in the mid-60s make this an excellent place to camp. However, one of the disadvantages of staying on this lake is that there are two private lots on the west shore which were severed in 1980 from a former summer resort. For this reason, I much prefer to stay on the more isolated Sucker Lake.

A small pothole can be found along the west shoreline of Bottle Lake. This glacial gouge and other important geological formations are what made the Ministry of Natural Resources turn this area into a nature reserve in the first place.

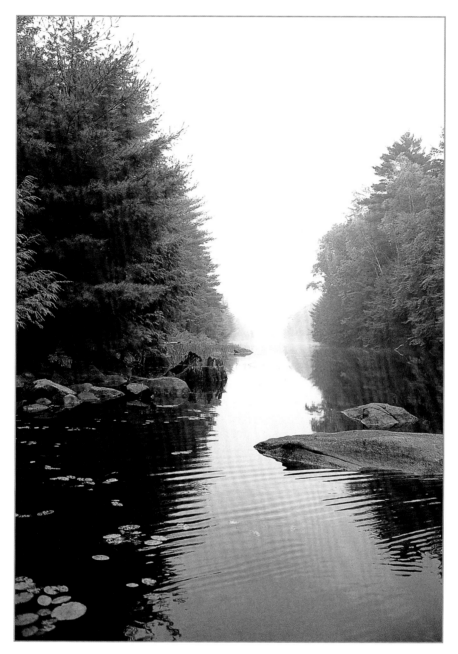

*Cedars and patches of purple iris grow along the banks of Bottle Creek.*

If you decide to portage into Sucker Lake, head east along the long inlet, then paddle north. To the left of the larger island located on the south end, take note of a smaller rock outcrop that I've nicknamed Laurel and Hardy Island due to a short, stubby pine growing next to a tall, skinny one.

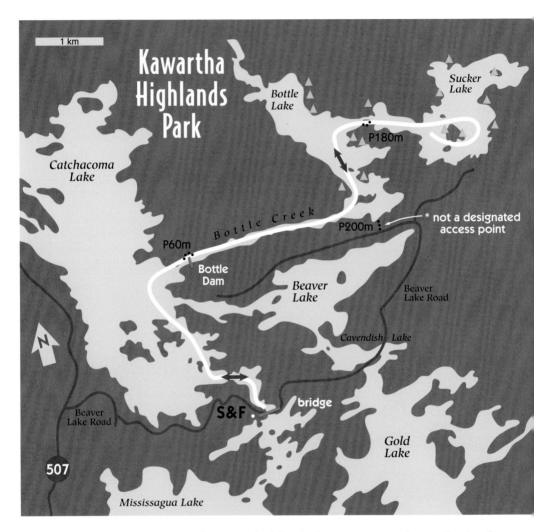

Of the four designated sites on the lake, the best camp is on the north side of the large island. The campsite on Laurel and Hardy Island may be a great place to catch a breeze, but it's far too small to survive constant use by canoeists.

Along the shores of Sucker Lake, a colony of rare meadow-beauty can be seen. Also found growing in the area is the rare primrose-leaved violet.

Sucker Lake has been designated a sensitive area by the MNR because it supports a good, natural lake trout fishery. This fishery is easier to monitor now that the area's status has been changed from a natural reserve to a provincial park. It will also help to preserve the sensitive site for future generations.

To return to the Catchacoma Lake access point, follow the same route. The trip will take approximately 2½ hours.

*Enjoying the last hours of daylight on Bottle Lake.*

# KAWARTHA HIGHLANDS PARK

**TIME** 1–2 days

**DIFFICULTY** This is a perfect novice route.

**NUMBER OF PORTAGES** 2 (both of which must be doubled back on)

**LONGEST PORTAGE** 200 yards (180 m)

**FEE** This is a non-operating provincial park and no fee is required.

**ALTERNATIVE ACCESS** A small parking area is located further along Beaver Lake Road, where a short portage can be taken down to Bottle Lake. Take note, however, that this is not a proper access point.

**FISH SPECIES** Catchacoma, Bottle and Sucker Lakes provide fair fishing for lake trout and both are excellent for bass fishing.

**ALTERNATIVE ROUTE** No

**KAYAK FRIENDLY** Yes

**OUTFITTERS**
WILD ROCK OUTFITTERS
169 Charlotte Street
Peterborough, Ontario
K9J 2T7
705-745-9133

ADVENTURE FITNESS
Buckhorn Road & County Road 18
R.R. 3
Lakefield, Ontario
K0L 2H0
705-652-7986

**FOR MORE INFORMATION**
MINISTRY OF NATURAL RESOURCES
Bancroft District Office
Box 500
Bancroft, Ontario
K0L 1C0
613-332-3940

**TOPOGRAPHIC MAP** 31 D/9

# Serpentine Lake Loop

**IMAGINE A CHAIN OF LAKES** smack dab in the middle of the north Kawartha region, complete with cascading waterfalls, perfect island campsites, stout pine trees, and excellent fishing. To be honest, when I first discovered the Serpentine route, I wanted to keep it all to myself. But eventually I couldn't stand to keep such a perfect paddle loop a secret.

This gem of a canoe route starts off from Anstruther Lake, just south of the town of Apsley. To reach the access point, turn left off Highway 28 onto Anstruther Road. Travel the rolling side road for approximately 6.25 miles (10 km) and as the main road veers to the left, take the marked dirt road straight down to the government boat-launching site on Anstruther Lake.

From the access point, paddle north, up Anstruther until the lake narrows. After the shallow channel, head northwest to the first portage, located past a group of small rocky islands and to the left of the trickling waterfalls. The 177-yard (162 m) path takes you over land from Anstruther to the more secluded Rathtun Lake. Campsites are available on the two islands in the middle of the lake and many canoeists choose to set up base camp on one of these isles. I much prefer to continue traveling northwest toward North Rathtun Lake.

At the end of Rathbun's far northwestern bay, a portage follows alongside a small creek for 148 yards (135 m) and leads into North Rathbun. Up until this point the forest cover consists of mixed stands of hardwood with a few stands of pine, hemlock and stunted oak rooted on exposed granite. From here, though, it changes to patches of spruce and tamarack growing through floating sphagnum mats. Where the sphagnum spreads across North Rathbun's southern shoreline, both of Canada's carnivorous plants, the sundew and pitcher plant, capture tiny insects to battle the bog's nutrient deficiency. The lake's northern shoreline is characterized by a large stand of white birch. These deciduous trees are beautiful during fall, with their bright yellow foliage crowning straight white trunks.

Otters frequent the waters of North Rathbun. While canoeing with friends from the city, I came upon the largest otter I've ever seen on this lake. It was playfully swimming close to my friends' canoe, but every time I went to point it out to them, the sly creature dove under their canoe and popped up on the opposite side. If my canoe partner hadn't verified my sighting, they would never have believed me.

The portage leading out of North Rathbun to Serpentine Lake is located by a natural sandy beach to the northeast. Before you get any ideas about taking a swim at the beach, however, I should warn you that in the past I've found North

*Miniature waterfall along the portage between Anstruther Lake and Rathbun Lake.*

Rathbun's waters to be leech-infested. But if the sun is out, you may want to risk it. If you do, have some salt handy on shore. If you sprinkle salt on leeches, they will usually loosen their grip.

Both Rathbun and North Rathbun lakes are named after a lumber baron who operated in the area. Just to the right of the portage, hidden among the brush close to where a creek enters North Rathbun, evidence of the area's logging era can be found. Among the treasures left behind are a tramway that once crossed a rocky crevice, and an old crosscut saw still bound in the trunk of a hemlock tree.

The portage to Serpentine is the longest on the route. It starts off on a groomed trail, then heads over patches of bare rock and through a woodland swamp. The most difficult portion of the 1,732-yard (1,584 m) pathway is at its end, where the portage works its way down a fairly steep grade. Now you know why I travel clockwise rather than counterclockwise on the loop.

*Serpentine Lake*

P1584m

*North Rathbun Lake*

P160m  P30m

*Copper Lake*

lift-over

P135m

*Rathbun Creek*

*Rathbun Lake*

P360m

P180m  *Anstruther Creek*

P162m

Rathbun Dam

N

1 km

*Anstruther Lake Road*

S&F

*Anstruther Lake*

marina

**Serpentine Lake Loop**

Because of the heavy minerals in the Serpentine Lake area, the water has a rusty tinge and at times a foul stench lingers in the air. Apart from the bad odor, however, Serpentine is the best lake to make camp on. Two excellent sites, one on an island to the south and the other on a point to the northeast, are equipped with a firepit and a canopy of red and white pine.

To finish the canoe loop, paddle to Serpentine's southern bay, where a creek flows out of the lake. A portage is marked to the right of the creek and runs alongside it for 175 yards (160 m), until the waterway becomes deep enough to navigate with the canoe. Wend your way through the twisting creek until you are forced out of the canoe once more to make a 33–yard (30 m) portage. After portaging, continue to follow the creek — lined with wild low-lying shrubs, clusters of wild iris, pickerel weed and the odd tamarack — until you come to where it enters Copper Lake. Depending on the water level, you may have to line or lift the canoe over into the lake's western bay.

The next portage, leading out of Copper Lake, is located at the southern tip of the opposite bay. The 394-yard (360 m) path heads up an ATV trail for approximately 22 yards (20 m), and then makes a sharp left turn, leading you through a mixed woodland and then down a steep grade to yet another shallow creek. It's essential to note that halfway along the portage the path cuts through another ATV trail. Make sure you don't go down the wrong path. I once found a family of four who had been lost for over an hour, having taken the wrong trail. Of course, I encountered the lost campers because I too had gone off in the wrong direction.

Joining Copper Lake with the familiar Rathbun Lake is an extensive marshland. Follow the creek, which snakes through the cattails and leatherleaf shrubs. You may have to stand up in the canoe to navigate through this lush wetland.

The marsh is home to dozens of red-winged blackbird families, but they're not the only species in abundance. On a hot summer day, I was quietly paddling through the cattails, heading for the portage into Rathbun, when I heard a faint sound of bells in the wind. At first I thought I was going bush happy; then, as I rounded a bend in the creek, I saw a herd of cows grazing in the wetland. Each one had a bell dangling from its neck, except for a solitary bull, who didn't seem to appreciate me gliding by his harem. I later discovered the cows belonged to a local farmer out on Highway 28 who leaves his livestock to graze freely throughout the area. Come the end of summer, each cow eventually wanders back to the barn, most having been impregnated by the contented bull.

The next year I traveled through the same place with friends from the city. Already aware of the "wild" cows, I enjoyed keeping them a secret and amused myself by allowing my chums to puzzle over what appeared to be huge moose patties along the portage (though the farmer is no longer allowed to have his cows graze in the area).

At the end of the marsh, the creek rushes over a beaver dam and marked to the left is a 200-yard (180 m) portage leading to Rathbun Lake. A beautiful waterfall can be seen halfway along the portage. This is one of the most scenic sights of the entire loop. With the cold water tumbling over moss-covered granite, you can't help but put down your gear and cool off under the cataract.

The portage ends where the creek enters Rathbun Lake. To finish your two days on the Serpentine Loop, paddle the length of the eastern inlet and head for the familiar portage into Anstruther, almost directly across the lake. To reach the access, return via the same route across Anstruther Lake. And remember, if you return the next year with friends, keep Serpentine's cows a secret until your partners spot a giant patty or two.

## SERPENTINE LAKE LOOP

**TIME** 2 days

**DIFFICULTY** A moderate level of canoe tripping skills is needed.

**NUMBER OF PORTAGES** 6 (1 which must be doubled back on)

**LONGEST PORTAGE** 1,732 yards (1,584 m)

**FEE** The Serpentine Lake Loop is situated in a non-operating park and no fee is required.

**ALTERNATIVE ACCESS** Marina, either right or left of the public access point.

**ALTERNATIVE ROUTE** It's possible to eliminate the long portage from North Rathburn to Serpentine by simply paddling/ portaging in and out of Serpentine by way of Rathbun–Anstruther Creek–Copper Lake.

**FISH SPECIES** Anstruther Lake and Rathbun Lake have fair fishing for lake trout, Rathbun and Copper Lake has a small population of walleye, and all lakes provide good bass fishing.

**KAYAK FRIENDLY** Only Rathbun Lake makes for an easy destination lake for kayakers.

**OUTFITTERS**
WILD ROCK OUTFITTERS
169 Charlotte Street
Peterborough, Ontario
K9J 2T7
705-745-9133

ADVENTURE FITNESS
Buckhorn Road & County Road 18
R.R. 3
Lakefield, Ontario
K0L 2H0
705-652-7986

**FOR MORE INFORMATION**
MINISTRY OF NATURAL RESOURCES
Bancroft District Office
Box 500
Bancroft, Ontario
K0L 1C0
613-332-3940

**TOPOGRAPHIC MAP** 31 D/9

# Crab Lake

**NOEL'S REQUESTS WERE QUITE DEMANDING** for his son's first canoe trip. He wanted a quick and easy route only a couple of hours drive from his home near Guelph; maybe a short portage so five-year-old Walker could experience, for a brief moment, what it felt to shoulder all your belongings on your back; and a choice campsite set on a remote lake that happens to be populated by monster-sized bass. Noel (the editor for my publishing company) had been on a number of trips with me before and I knew he wouldn't be at all surprised to hear that such a perfect trip didn't exist. But it did. A place called Crab Lake. And it's a gem I couldn't wait to share with him and Walker.

Crab Lake can be reached by Wolf Lake, which has an access point on its far eastern end. To reach the launch site, turn left off Highway 28, just south of Apsley, and onto Anstruther Lake Road. Then, just over 3 miles (exactly 5 km) along, an unmarked dirt road to the left will lead you down to Wolf Lake. It seems like a relatively easy process, but because the last road is not marked, you can easily find yourself lost. Our group missed the turn for Wolf Lake twice and even somehow managed to begin paddling across a totally different lake for half an hour before we realized our mistake. We then resorted to asking a local cottager to steer us in the right direction.

Wolf Lake is a perfect destination on its own. Only a few cottages crowd the lake, mostly along the south shore, and a strip of Crown land along the north shore, as well as a number of small islands to the west, provide some excellent campsite possibilities. Crab Lake is much more isolated, however, and is easily reached by way of a short, 117-yard (107 m) portage. The take-out is located at the far end of Wolf Lake's southwest bay, just before the last two cottages along the south shore.

Crab Lake has five main bays that head off in all directions (therefore its local name, Star Lake) and is much larger than it first appears. Each inlet also has one or two prime campsites, complete with an exposed chunk of granite to catch a breeze on to escape the bugs and a snug canopy of pine, maple and birch to pitch a tent under. Our group chose an out-of-the-way spot directly below where a rough trail heads up to the top of Blueberry Mountain (an exposed hill that's literally covered in thick blueberry bushes) and, after quickly setting up camp, we headed out in the canoe again in search of the lake's monster bass.

We cast our lines out the moment we entered the first weedy bay; Noel and I with our fancy plugs and spinners, and Walker with his half-dead worm stuck on a bare hook. It was my idea to give Walker the defunct bait, thinking the lake's

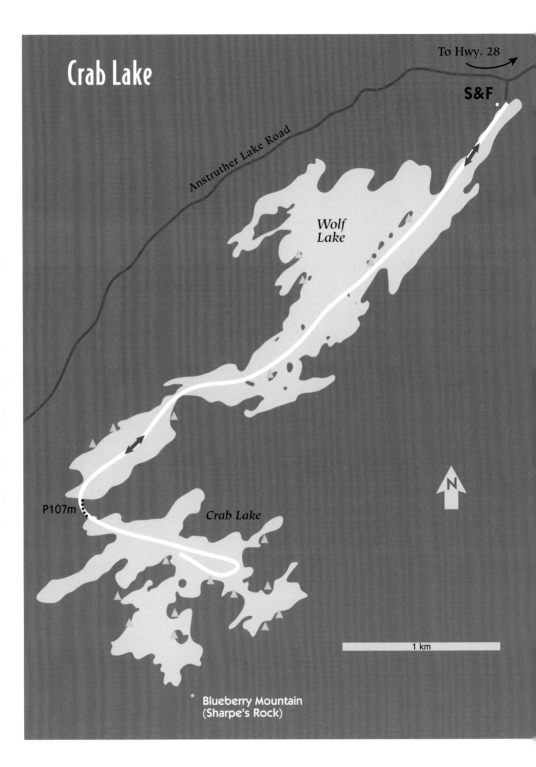

Crab Lake

To Hwy. 28

S&F

Anstruther Lake Road

*Wolf Lake*

*Crab Lake*

P107m

N

1 km

Blueberry Mountain
(Sharpe's Rock)

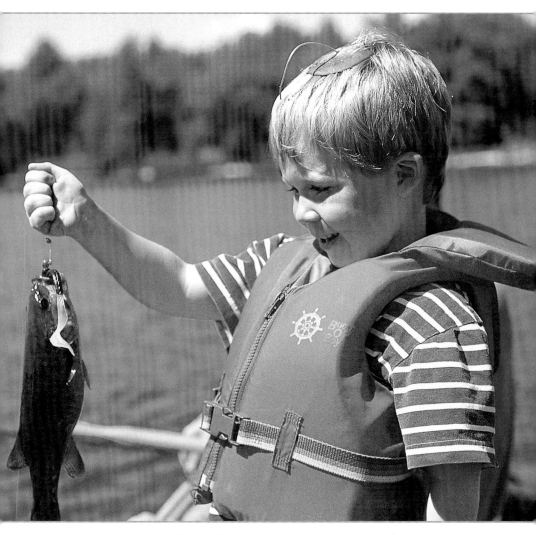

*"Here's another one, Dad." (Walker "Bass Master" Hudson, Crab Lake)*

healthy population of sunfish would keep him occupied for at least long enough for Noel and me to catch some decent-sized bass for supper. Of course, in no time at all, Walker had caught three bass, averaging around four pounds each, and Noel and I hadn't even had a single bite. Quickly we switched to the decomposing worms and, in exchange, allowed Walker full rein on our lure boxes. Ten minutes later Walker had caught two more trophy bass (one on my scent-impregnated rubber frog and the other on Noel's pink-colored "Holla-Popper"). Noel and I still remained fishless.

I doubt that this lake had ever given up so many fish. In fact, Noel and I were quite mystified by Walker's success and had to blame it on beginners' luck to settle our egos. Walker, on the other hand, had a different reason for catching so many lunkers. Each time he lowered his line into the water, the intrepid angler would whisper a secret code: "Here fishy, fishy, fishy." Walker was insistent that without saying this magical phrase, no fish would ever bite the hook. So, we agreed to play along for the fun of it — or maybe we were just that desperate to catch a fish — and both tossed out our lines and repeated the expression "Here fishy, fishy, fishy." Ten minutes later Noel and I had caught a couple of bass each.

Thinking back, the trip to Crab Lake wasn't a complete success, not according to Noel's criteria. The route was actually two-and-a-half hours' drive from his home; Walker only carried his personal pack halfway along the portage before handing it over to his father; and Noel and I never did catch a trophy bass. It did manage to fulfill his main objective, though — Walker can't wait until next years' trip — and according to Noel, a father can't ask for anything more perfect than that.

## CRAB LAKE

**DIFFICULTY** Novice

**PORTAGES** 1

**LONGEST PORTAGE** 117 yards (107 m)

**FEE** Crab Lake is an unmaintained provincial park and no fee is required.

**ALTERNATIVE ACCESS** None

**ALTERNATIVE ROUTE** Some canoeists prefer to stay on one of the Crown land sites on Wolf Lake.

**FISH SPECIES** Wolf Lake has a good population of muskellunge, and both Wolf Lake and Crab Lake offer good bass fishing.

**KAYAK FRIENDLY** Yes

**OUTFITTERS**
WILD ROCK OUTFITTERS
169 Charlotte Street
Peterborough, Ontario
K9J 2T7
705-745-9133

ADVENTURE FITNESS
Buckhorn Road & County Road 18
R.R. 3
Lakefield, Ontario
K0L 2H0
705-652-7986

**FOR MORE INFORMATION**
MINISTRY OF NATURAL RESOURCES
Bancroft District Office Box 500
Bancroft, Ontario
K0L 1C0
613-332-3940

**TOPOGRAPHICAL MAP**
Burleigh Falls 31 D/9

# Long Lake Loop

**ALL PADDLERS HAVE THAT MEMORABLE ROUTE** that holds special meaning in their lives. Mine was a trip through the Long Lake Loop during a July weekend in the early 1980s. That calm Saturday morning in the north Kawarthas, I pushed off from the same shore as my canoe companions and I had set out from in previous years, except this trip was a little different — this time I headed out alone.

The solo weekend wasn't planned; I would have loved my regular canoe mates to have tagged along, but a few days before our departure, they had all been forced to cancel out. At first I was upset with them for abandoning me. But after the trip was over and I realized that the solo adventure had dramatically changed my life as a canoeist, I was grateful to them.

In any case, the Long Lake Loop is perfect for a group trip or for going solo. To reach the access point, drive north from Woodview along Highway 28 and make a left onto Long Lake Road. Long Lake Lodge is situated at the end of the road, and for a few dollars the owners will allow you to park your vehicle in their lot. If you arrive late on a Friday night or before 8 A.M. on a Saturday, plan to pay on your return. Launch your canoe from the beach and head directly across the entire length of Long Lake, which is appropriately named.

A long, narrow channel joins the western arm of Long Lake with Loucks Lake. Loucks is the first of six interconnecting lakes that I prefer to explore in a counterclockwise direction. At the far western end of Loucks, there are two marked portages. To travel the route counterclockwise, use the 145-yard (133 m) portage to your right. The path cuts between a cottage to the left and a rock out-crop to the right. From the rickety old dock at the end of the portage, go west, following a shallow, rock-strewn stream toward Cox Lake. You will see that the stream is bordered by alder and willow, and populated by "meowing" catbirds. Halfway along to Cox, the forest cover changes from oak and birch to pine and hemlock. Depending on the water level, you may have to lift your canoe over dry sections of the stream.

Just before Cox Lake, the stream becomes impossible to navigate and you must use the marked 33-yard (30 m) portage to Cox Lake. This portage, like many on the route, is lined with patches of poison ivy, so keep your eyes peeled for the three-leaved plant growing on the forest floor. If you happen to acciden-tally step on it, look down by the stream for touch-me-not (spotted jewelweed), which can be identified by its spotted orange flowers. This plant usually grows beside poison ivy, and if you rub its juices on your skin shortly after coming in

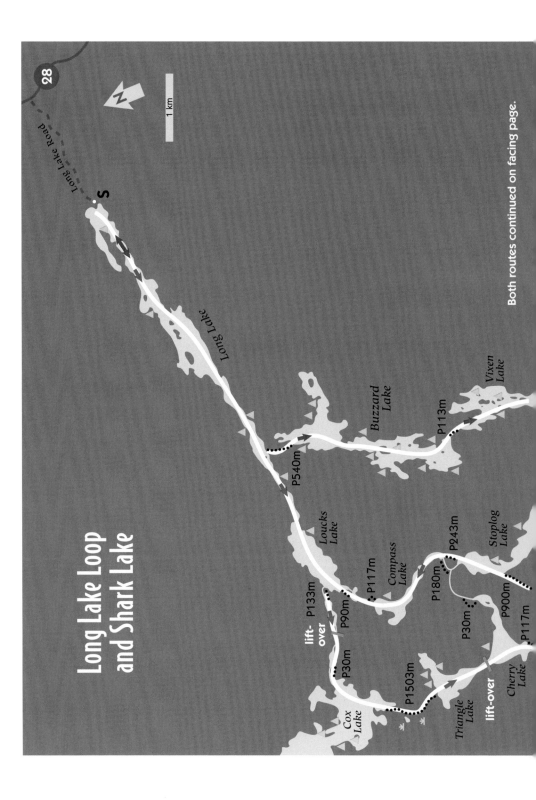

# Long Lake Loop and Shark Lake

28

Long Lake Road

S

Long Lake

1 km

P540m

Buzzard Lake

Vixen Lake

P113m

Loucks Lake

Compass Lake

Stoplog Lake

P117m

P243m

lift-over

P133m

P90m

P180m

P30m

P30m

P900m

P117m

P1503m

Cox Lake

Triangle Lake

lift-over

Cherry Lake

Both routes continued on facing page.

Both routes continued from facing page.

Big
Cedar
Lake

28

Coon Lake Road

**F**

Coon
Lake

Shark
Lake

P22m

P990m

P765m

Vixen
Lake

Buzzard
Creek

P22m

P990m

Stoplog
Lake

P900m

Turtle
Lake

P117m

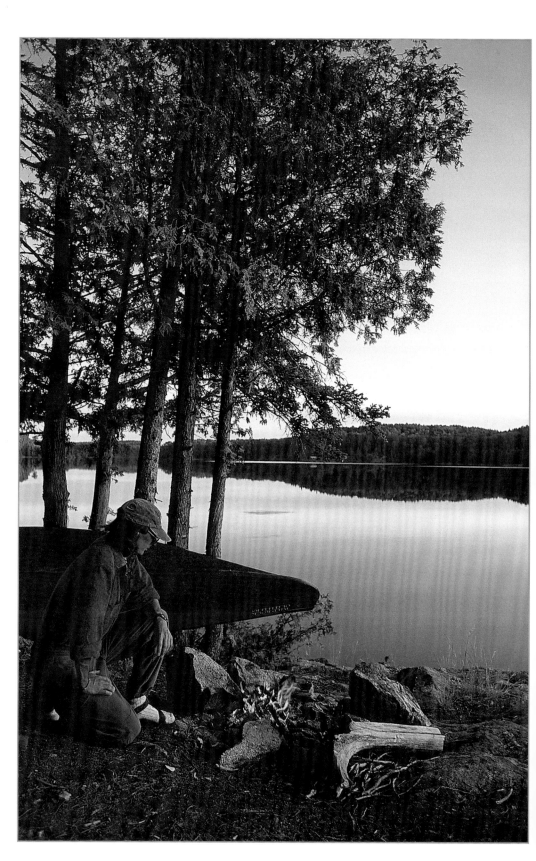

contact with poison ivy, you may eliminate the burning itch. Juices from the touch-me-not are also effective in soothing the itch of bug bites.

Head out onto scenic Cox Lake, making your way to the southern bay, just past the isolated cabin used by deer hunters in the fall. There you will find the lengthy portage to Triangle Lake. The 1,643-yard (1,503 m) path is the longest portage on this loop, and after you have carried your gear down the steep grade at the trail's end, you will thank me for having suggested that you travel counter-clockwise. Note that the path crosses an ATV trail, so try not to wander off in the wrong direction. If it's still reasonably early by the time you get to Triangle Lake, take time out to fish for bass or to climb up on the rocky shoreline and collect a basket of blueberries for the next day's breakfast.

Triangle Lake joins Cherry Lake by way of a short, shallow channel where a lift-over may be necessary. From Cherry Lake you have two options. You can either head to the east, shortening the loop by two lakes (Turtle and Stoplog), or if beavers have dried up the channel to the east, you may be better off paddling directly across the lake to the south. Here a 128-yard (117 m) portage leads into Turtle Lake. I've tried both options and prefer the latter.

Turtle Lake is rarely used and there's a nice island campsite. However, you may want to portage the 984 yards (900 m) into Stoplog Lake before retiring for the night. The portage is a little buggy, making its way through a lowland spruce and sphagnum swamp and then up and down a rock uprise, but the tent sites are inviting and the fishing is great.

Stoplog Lake is where I camped when I traveled the Long Lake Loop solo. I pitched my tent south of the portage, just before the tapered inlet. I first chose a designated site along the eastern shore, but as I searched the backwoods behind my tent for firewood, I came across a phoebe nestling camouflaged on the forest floor. The little one was calling out for Mom. I watched to see if the mother would return to feed her young, and when she did, I gathered my gear and left the site to the flustered flycatcher family.

That night, as I sat by the fire alone in the wilds, the sounds were deafening. Dozens of whippoorwills called out as they snatched up flying insects, and the eastern screech owl uttered its series of quavering whistles, descending in pitch. There were times when I questioned my sanity. I spent the first part of the night curled up in the fetal position, wide awake and jumping at the night sounds. But every time I felt spooked, I reminded myself how many others had traveled alone before me and gained insight from solitude. That realization marked a turning point in my emotions. Complete loneliness was suddenly transformed into a sense of freedom, an invigorating and exciting awareness of the life around as

*A quiet night alone on Stoplog Lake.*

well as within me. It didn't take long before every little noise that had kept me awake was soon lulling me to sleep.

To finish the Long Lake Loop, you must push or pole your canoe through the weed-infested north end of Stoplog to locate the 266-yard (243 m) portage into the shallows preceding Compass Lake. The portage runs up a steep bank alongside cascading water, passes by a small hunting cabin and then goes down to a giant beaver dam. Paddle north through the shallows and take another portage (200 yards [180 m]) into Compass Lake. Two more portages (128 yards and 99 yards [117 m, 90 m]) are necessary to make your way through the shallows and back to the familiar Loucks Lake, then to Long Lake. Once you return to Long Lake, you will have completed a perfect loop through the heart of the north Kawarthas.

## LONG LAKE LOOP

**TIME** 2–3 days

**DIFFICULTY** A moderate level of canoe tripping experience is needed.

**NUMBER OF PORTAGES** 8

**LONGEST PORTAGE** 1,643 yards (1,503 m)

**FEE** The Long Lake Loop is situated in a non-operating park and no fee is required.

**ALTERNATIVE ACCESS** No

**ALTERNATIVE ROUTE** Portages into Stoplog Lake and Turtle Lake can be eliminated by taking a 197-yard (180 m) portage and 33-yard (30 m) portage on the north side of the creek leading into Cherry Lake.

**FISH SPECIES** Long Lake has a small population of lake trout, and bass fishing is good throughout the entire route.

**KAYAK FRIENDLY** No

**OUTFITTERS**
WILD ROCK OUTFITTERS
169 Charlotte Street
Peterborough, Ontario
K9J 2T7
705-745-9133

ADVENTURE FITNESS
Buckhorn Road & County Road 18
R.R. 3
Lakefield, Ontario
K0L 2H0
705-652-7986

**FOR MORE INFORMATION**
MINISTRY OF NATURAL RESOURCES
Bancroft District Office
Box 500
Bancroft, Ontario
K0L 1C0
613-332-3940

**TOPOGRAPHIC MAP** 31 D/9

# Shark Lake

**OVER 2,000 CANOEISTS** visit the Long Lake area every year, and at times the portages can seem overwhelmingly busy. There is a way to avoid the crowds, however. Instead of paddling the chain of lakes west of Long Lake, canoe south, down a number of connecting lakes (including scenic Shark Lake), to the government dock on Coon Lake. The hassle of shuttling a vehicle to the Coon Lake access point is about the only disadvantage to this enjoyable two-day route.

To leave a second vehicle at the pick-up site, turn left off Highway 28 onto Coon Lake Road, 1 mile (1.6 km) north of Burleigh Falls. Then take the first left and park your car where the road loops around like a court in an urban subdivision.

To reach the access point on Long Lake, drive north along Highway 28 and turn left onto Long Lake Road. The put-in spot is the same as the one for the previously mentioned Long Lake route. Push off the sandy beach and paddle west, down the length of Long Lake. Before you reach the narrow channel joining Long and Loucks Lakes, portage into Buzzard Lake. The 590-yard (540 m) portage is situated along the southern shoreline and can be easily recognized by a wooden dock in front of an old hunter's shack. The locals call Buzzard Lake Trout Lake, but the former name is the more appropriate one, as sightings of turkey vultures are common, while the lake's trout population is almost non-existent.

To reach the more secluded Shark Lake, paddle the length of Buzzard and take the relatively easy 124-yard (113 m) portage into Vixen Lake. The path begins at Buzzard Lake's most southerly end. Head south once again, canoeing the entire length of Vixen Lake, and then portage a third time to reach Shark Lake. This portage is not as easy as the previous one. Its 837-yard (765 m) length does, however, take you farther into the wilds of the Kawarthas.

The pine and hemlock that dominated the shoreline of Buzzard and the north bay of Vixen are now replaced by mixed second growth. The valleys are ruled by birch and maple, with the odd stand of pine, hemlock and yellow birch. The landscape is more open in this area as well, and the exposed granite ridges are excellent places to spot deer, attracted by the foliage of stunted oak trees, and even bears browsing on patches of blueberries.

There are three marked campsites on Shark. The island site to the southeast or the site along a beautiful natural sandy beach to the northeast are my favorites. Both are perfect for swimming and watching the sun set.

A long, steady 1,082-yard (990 m) portage leads out of Shark Lake from its southern bay to the first of three small unnamed connecting lakes. Two 24-yard (22 m) portages join the lakes, with a short paddle between them. The grass along the banks of the creeks that trickle in and out of the small lakes grows higher than canoeists heads, but provide excellent spots to sight otters, ducks, mink, great blue herons, and even broad-winged and sharp-shinned hawks.

The beginning of the final portage is located at the southern end of the last unnamed lake. (This is a great place to view loons.) The 1,082-yard (990 m) path to Coon Lake slowly climbs up a rise, bordered by the forest type seen at the start of the trip, crosses over a cottage road and then heads down a steep grade to the lake. A 20-minute paddle down the southern inlet of Coon Lake will take you to the government dock and end your trip along the Shark Lake route.

# SHARK LAKE

**TIME** 2 days

**DIFFICULTY** A moderate level of canoe tripping experience is needed.

**NUMBER OF PORTAGES** 7

**LONGEST PORTAGE** 1,082 yards (990 m)

**FEE** The Shark Lake route is situated in a non-operating park, and no fee is required.

**ALTERNATIVE ACCESS** No

**ALTERNATIVE ROUTE** It is possible to shorten the trip to eliminate a car shuttle by either paddling/portaging from Long Lake to Buzzard Lake (returning via the same route) or from Coon Lake to Shark Lake (returning via the same route).

**FISH SPECIES** Long Lake and Buzzard Lake have fair fishing for lake trout, and bass fishing is good throughout the entire route.

**KAYAK FRIENDLY** No. However, it is possible to use a wheel cart to transport your kayak along the portage from Long Lake to Buzzard Lake.

**OUTFITTERS**

WILD ROCK OUTFITTERS
169 Charlotte Street
Peterborough, Ontario
K9J 2T7
705-745-9133

ADVENTURE FITNESS
Buckhorn Road & County Road 18
R.R. 3
Lakefield, Ontario
K0L 2H0
705-652-7986

**FOR MORE INFORMATION**

MINISTRY OF NATURAL RESOURCES
Bancroft District Office
Box 500
Bancroft, Ontario
K0L 1C0
613-332-3940

**TOPOGRAPHIC MAP** 31 D/9

# Eels Creek

**AS YOU CANOE THE TWISTING EELS CREEK** down toward Stony Lake, you are not only able to view a remarkable transition between two distinct natural habitats, but you also have the opportunity to canoe down a historic waterway used by Algonkian shamans over 1,000 years ago.

The trip begins where the creek flows under Highway 28, north of Burleigh Falls, past the town of Woodview, and ends just before Eels flows into Stony, by the bridge on Northey's Bay Road. The first day is spent on the creek, paddling all the way to High Falls. This gives you most of day two to hike from your campsite at the falls to Petroglyphs Provincial Park.

Before putting in upstream, you must first drive a second vehicle to the route's end. From Highway 28 turn right onto Northey's Bay Road, just past the town of Woodview. (Look for a road sign for Petrogylphs Provincial Park.) Park your car north of the bridge crossing over Eels Creek, then drive back along Northey's Bay Road to Highway 28. Turn right onto the highway and head for the access point, where the creek flows under the highway, just a few minutes' drive up the road. Immediately after the bridge on Highway 28, make a left onto the dirt road or a right onto a small pull-over area. The old homestead, which was once a put-in spot, can no longer be used, so canoeists must begin directly below the bridge.

The moment you paddle past the highway bridge, the first of the two forest types presents itself — dense second growth, with shrubby swamps and thick soft-maple stands. Black ducks and wood ducks ("woodies") flush as you round each bend, and the odd white-tailed deer bounds from its bed of ferns along the creek's banks. Almost 2 miles (3 km) downstream, you will come to the first portage, a 20-yard (18 m) lift-over to the left of a small falls, where the ferns are replaced by bunchberry and trailing arbutus, and red and white pine rooted in rugged granite dominate soft-maple swamps. The creek passes through the northern sphere, cutting through stone banks, forced by the rigidity of bedrock to discipline its course. Less than a mile downstream, a sharp bend in the creek speeds up the flow enough that you may have to portage to avoid a short stretch of rapids. The creek quickens over a stunted cataract once more before reaching High Falls, with the portage (60 yards [54 m]) running along the right-hand side.

You'll hear the roar of High Falls long before you see it. Designated campsites are marked on both banks before the drop (and a 177-yard [162 m] portage is on the left). The site on top of a rocky platform along the right bank is my favorite. The falls is a popular stopover spot, maybe too popular. So if you hear groups of campers loudly exclaiming their love of the great outdoors over the boom of the cascading water, I advise you to paddle back upstream and use a less crowded site.

Before Christopher Columbus "discovered" America, Algonkian shamans beached their birchbark canoes above High Falls and headed east, into the land of spirits. I strongly suggest you rise early the next morning and hike along the almost 3-mile (4.5 km) trail to Petroglyphs Provincial Park to visit the Algonkians' spiritual monument. The large crystalline limestone panel of prehistoric picture-writing symbols is probably one of the most unique finds of Native petroglyphs in Canada. The site was discovered in 1954 by a group of American Nepheline Mines employees. The general manager, Ernest Craig, and his colleagues, Charles Phipps and Everitt Davis, stumbled upon the carvings while taking an afternoon break on top of the exposed rock. The more than 900 petroglyphs represent the visions and religious yearnings of the various Algonkian shamans who gathered here. The symbols they sketched in the soft rock depict many forms: shaman figures, phallic symbols, evil serpents, soul-boats that the shamans used while in search of wandering souls in other worlds,

*The first half of Eel's Creek offers a unique forest type of dense second growth with shrubby swamps and thick soft-maple stands.*

the mother earth in the form of a turtle, and the single most significant glyph, Kitchi Manitou, the Great Spirit itself.

The exact meaning of the petroglyphs is not yet totally understood. Joan and Roman Vastokas explained it best in their book, *Sacred Art of the Algonkians*, when they wrote, "The images engraved here are not the projections of man imposing his will upon his surroundings. Instead, they render visible the hidden meanings in nature whose significance it has been the shaman's task to conjure up and capture on stone."

The petroglyph site is now protected by a giant seven-sided building that has generated a certain amount of controversy. Some say if it weren't for the building, the carvings, exposed to the elements, would disappear within 15 years. Yet those Natives who believe the sky is one route to creation contend that the roof over the site is blocking that route and that the spirits cannot roam freely between earth and sky. Some even believe that a very powerful force has been trapped inside and is struggling to free itself.

The round trip from High Falls to the park and back takes about four hours. Once you've hiked back to High Falls and packed your gear, it takes less than an hour to paddle from the falls to the bridge on Northey's Bay Road. Three short portages are necessary along the route. The first is located on the left, alongside High Falls. The next is to the left of a quick drop from the pond below the falls to a second lower pond. And the final portage is also situated on the left bank along a rocky uprise. If water levels permit, the last set of rapids, and possibly the second to last set, can be run without difficulty.

Once you have spent a weekend paddling down this historic route, you will realize why canoeists who have traveled through Eels Creek regard it as one of the few waterways in cottage country that can link us to the mystic past of the native people. To me, canoeing down Eels Creek to view the shamans' carvings is like walking down the church aisle toward the sacred altar.

## EELS CREEK

**TIME** 1–2 days

**DIFFICULTY** This is considered a novice route but some experience in white water canoeing is needed.

**NUMBER OF PORTAGES** 6

**LONGEST PORTAGE** 177 yards (162 m)

**FEE** Eels Creek is situated, for the most part, on Crown land, and no fee is needed for Canadian citizens.

**ALTERNATIVE ACCESS** None

**ALTERNATIVE ROUTE** To eliminate a car shuttle it is possible to simply paddle upstream to High Falls from the Northey's Bay Road access point, returning via the same route.

**FISH SPECIES** Bass can be caught along the entire river, and there is a small population of muskellunge between High Falls and Northey's Bay Road.

**KAYAK FRIENDLY** Only the alternative route

**OUTFITTERS**
WILD ROCK OUTFITTERS
169 Charlotte Street
Peterborough, Ontario
K9J 2T7
705-745-9133

ADVENTURE FITNESS
Buckhorn Road & County Road 18
R.R. 3
Lakefield, Ontario
K0L 2H0
705-652-7986

**FOR MORE INFORMATION**
MINISTRY OF NATURAL RESOURCES
Bancroft District Office
Box 500
Bancroft, Ontario
K0L 1C0
613-332-3940

**TOPOGRAPHIC MAP** 31 D/9

# Mississagua River

**EVERY RIVER HAS A CHARACTER OF ITS OWN,** but some have a more distinct personality than others. The Mississagua has a subtle charm that instantly bewitches the first-time river-runner and turns him or her into a lifetime white-water fanatic.

The river flows between Mississagua Lake and Buckhorn Lake. To access the river so as to leave behind a second vehicle, drive to where the Mississagua flows under Highway 36, just east of Buckhorn. Park your vehicle on the shoulder of the road, then drive north of Buckhorn, turning off toward Gooderham on Highway 507. From the 507 turn right onto Mississagua Dam Road. Follow the boat-launching signs for 2 miles (3 km) until you come to a parking area beside the dam. Take the 55-yard (50 m) portage from the lot to the base of the dam and the beginning of the Mississagua River. The waterway is open and shallow here, with cottages dotting the shore. Your paddle may frequently push into the sandy soil under the flow, digging up crayfish and clams.

The river soon changes character as it leaves the developed shorelines and begins to quicken its pace, flowing over a series of rocky staircases. Four sets of portages are presented in quick succession, ranging from approximately 50 yards to 186 yards (45–170 m). Due to the unavailability of detailed information on the Mississagua River route, all portage lengths are approximate. The first portage (186 yards [170 m]) is to the right and crosses a dirt road, avoiding a scenic split falls and a short swift flowing under a small bridge. Put in to the right of the bridge, paddle across a small pond and portage 50 yards (45 m) to the right, around the third stairway. Almost immediately after the second portage the river twists to the south and flushes through a rocky chute. Portage 99 yards (90 m) along the left bank, or if you feel a little adventurous and the water levels and your experience are up to snuff, line the canoe through the chute on the right bank and then run the rapids. Steep granite walls run along this section and a boulder garden awaits you at the end, so remember, once started, you are committed. Even though this set of rapids is among the best on the river, if in doubt, choose the portage. The portage finishes near the base of the rapids. If water levels are low, you may want to paddle directly across from the first portage and use a second portage (50 yards [45 m]) on the left bank to avoid decorating the rocks with canoe paint. The fourth portage (88 yards [80 m]) is a little farther downstream and again is located to the left, passing over a section of private property.

After going under a snowmobile bridge, the river stretches out its banks and calms its flow. The last section of fast water is hardly noticeable and can easily be

# Mississagua River

*Mississagua Lake*

PR50m

**S**

*Mississagua Dam Rd.*

dam

*Gold Lake Road*

PR45m

PR 170m

PL 90m

iron bridge
**Alternative Access**

PL80m

*River*

PL60m **lift-over**

PL80m CBR

PL158m

PR50m

PL358m

PL257m

*Mississauga*

**507**

**36**

1 km

CBR =
Check Before
Running

PL40m CBR

PL20m CBR

PL216m

PR130m CBR

Route is continued at top of facing page.

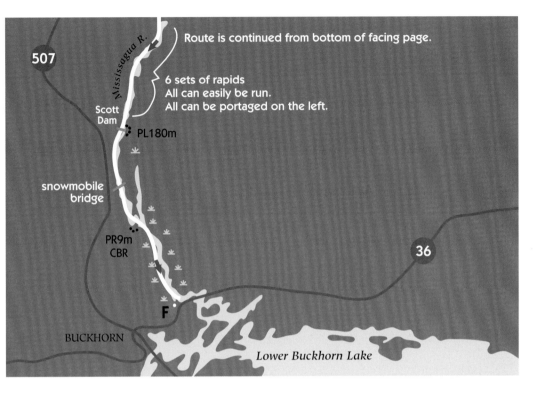

507

*Mississagua R.*

Route is continued from bottom of facing page.

6 sets of rapids
All can easily be run.
All can be portaged on the left.

Scott
Dam

PL180m

snowmobile
bridge

PR9m
CBR

36

F

BUCKHORN

*Lower Buckhorn Lake*

run. A 44-yard (40 m) portage is located to the right, however. During early spring, which is really the only time to run the Mississagua, the water along this section is alive with spawning suckers.

Since the river was once used to flush logs down to Buckhorn Lake and then down the Trent system, it is no wonder that the fish population has dwindled to schools of suckers, with the odd bass lurking in the lower, deeper pools. Along this shallow section, one can plunge the blade of one's paddle into the river's seemingly sandy bottom and disturb the bark and wood chips left behind by the giant pines that once tumbled down the swollen spring river. Today a patchwork of second growth has replaced the pines that once grew in the low-lying areas, and a crop of stunted oak carpets the rock-strewn landscape that bears little resemblance to the wasteland left by the loggers.

For 1.5 miles (2.5 km) the river moves slowly through a broad stretch of low, flooded vegetation. Mississauga natives once hunted and trapped in these calm sections. I remember paddling along this quiet section in late May one year and hearing baby beavers whimpering inside their lodge, pushed up against the eroded shoreline. As I drifted closer to the stick-and-mud structure, I was startled by the mother beaver, who swam directly under my canoe, emerged a few feet from my bow and then loudly slapped her tail against the surface of the water. I quickly acted upon her warning signal and paddled away from the lodge.

Eventually the surrounding scenery becomes more towering and a yellow portage marker appears on the left bank, indicating that the river once again drops down over hard granite. The first set of rapids can be lined and portaged or run by lifting your gear over the beginning chute. You should put in immediately after and then maneuver through a straight channel filled with swirling water and jagged rocks. By running the rapids, you avoid two portages (66 yards and 88 yards [60 m, 80 m] in length) marked along the rocks to the left, but make sure to check the waterway beforehand. Only a few yards downriver, another portage, 173 yards (158 m) long, is marked along the left bank. Don't miss it. The following set of rapids cannot be run unless you put in below where the river splits, forming three separate falls. By running or lining the last section, you can cut the portage in half.

A campsite that overlooks the triple falls is located along the portage, but I prefer to travel just a little farther and make camp at the most awe-inspiring site on the river. The Mississagua first tumbles over a steep ledge, down into a quiet pool, then crashes down a rocky gorge. A short portage (55 yards [50 m]) is marked to the right of the first falls, then a second portage (390 yards [358 m]) can be found almost immediately beside the first; just follow the shoreline to the western arm of the pool. To shorten this portage, the longest on the route, I simply paddle across the pool, keeping to the right of the second drop, then clamber up the rocky bank and bushwhack 22 yards (20 m) until I meet up with the end of the extensive portage. The picturesque campsite is off to the left of the portage, alongside the gorge. You can set up camp here.

The next morning you can enjoy a relaxed 2-mile (3 km) paddle through yet another meandering section of the river, which is interrupted halfway by a single set of rapids. The portage is marked to the left (280 yards [257 m]), but it is runnable if water levels permit.

Following the portage, the muddy banks are once again replaced with hard rock. Birch trees and trilliums give way to pine and columbine plants, and you'll soon hear the familiar roar of the river as it descends over granite. The next two portages are short (44 yards and 22 yards [40 m, 20 m]) and are marked along the left bank. You can easily run this section, but you must carry over the third set of rapids, using the 236-yard (216 m) trail located along the left bank.

I know what you're thinking: not another portage! Well, to be honest, the first time I looked at the Mississagua River route on a map and counted more than 20 portages over a 10-mile (16 km) stretch, I said forget it. But one early spring weekend my wife, Alana, talked me into attempting the river. We blindly set forth,

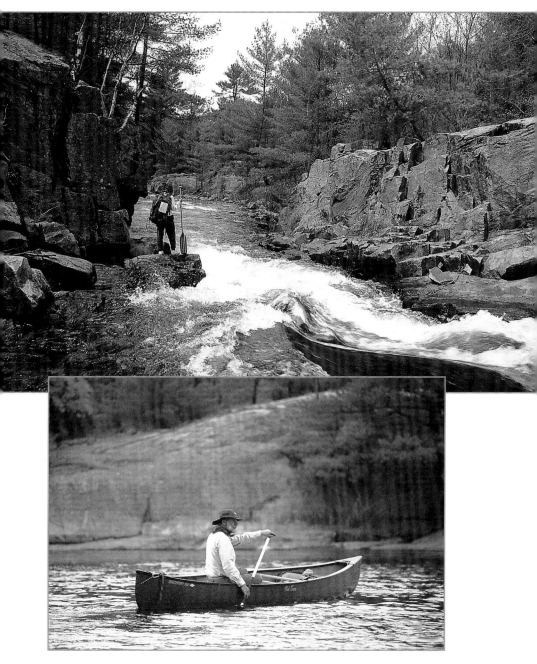

*Above: It's not long before the Mississagua River quickens its pace and begins to flow over a series of rocky staircases (Alana Callan). Below: Taking it easy between running rapids on the Mississagua (Len Lockwood).*

with little whitewater experience, and soon discovered the magic of the Mississagua.

From the put-in to the set of rapids shortly after the previously mentioned 236-yard (216 m) portage, the majority of the rapids are next to impossible to run. But as you make your way farther downstream, the rapids gradually become easier and easier. The magical part about all this is that while you are shooting more and more rapids, you think it's the skill you've gained along the way that has enabled you to conquer the river, not the ease of the runs themselves.

When Alana and I reached the halfway point, we came across a bend in the river where we could hear the roar of the rushing rapids just ahead. We went ashore so I could check the ease of the portage. After finding the 142-yard (130 m) trail was blazed through a bug-infested swamp, I opted to look to see if the rapids were runnable. From my vantage point on a rocky ledge, I could gaze down at the rapids. The river squeezed itself through a narrow, boulder-strewn canyon, creating a series of deep water haystack waves halfway through the run. But the boulder garden at the base of the rapids was swallowed by high water, so the only difficulty would lie in trying to balance the canoe through the haystacks.

I quickly returned to where Alana was holding the canoe and asked her if she wanted to attempt to run them. "Sure, let's go for it!" she exclaimed. So I tied down the packs, tucked my legs under my seat, zipped up my lifejacket and pushed off from shore, allowing the current to take us around the bend in the river.

The moment I saw the sudden drop and swirling water, a lump formed in my throat. The rapids sure seemed a lot safer from the rocky ledge along the portage than at the brink of the tumbling river.

"Back paddle, back paddle," I screamed to Alana at the bow. It was too late. The current dragged us into the gut of the rapids and pushed our flimsy fiber-glass vessel straight into the rolling haystacks. As the canoe bounced up and down the waves like a roller coaster, I began to panic. Luckily, with Alana still back paddling, I was able to shift the canoe away from the worst of it by making a series of pries and sculling draws. At the base of the rapids, a small eddy worked in our favor as we swung out of the rushing current to safety.

Before I was able to catch my breath and apologize to my bow partner for having chosen to run through all that foam and froth, Alana gave out a loud "Yaaa-hoooo!" and then asked, "Can we run it again?" There was nothing I could do for her now: The magical Mississagua had cast its spell and Alana was doomed to be a whitewater fanatic forever.

After the last set of rapids, the river tumbles over rock 12 more times. Most of these rapids can be run without difficulty in moderate water levels — all can be lined and or portaged if necessary), except for the rapids that plunge over the ruins of the old Scott's Mill dam. The dam is a cement structure that was built by W.A. Scott in 1870 to flush his licensed timber along the Mississagua River down to Buckhorn Lake. Ownership of the dam has changed several times over the years, and in 1928 the dam was sold to the federal government, who use it to control water levels. The historic site appears soon after the sixth rapid, where Alana and I fought foam and froth. To avoid the turbulent waters crashing over the dam, hug the left bank. A portage trail (200 yards [180 m]) begins well above the falls.

After you have navigated through the last section of whitewater (five sections in total, with only the fifth having a marked 10-yard [9 m] portage to the right), the Mississagua slows and appears more like a long lake than a raging river. The banks are thick with green growth: willow, alder, dogwood, leatherleaf and bog-laurel. Yellow warblers, cowbirds and eastern kingbirds can be seen among the foliage. Gradually the signs of civilization make their appearance, marking the end of a spellbinding trip down a magical river.

## MISSISSAGUA RIVER

**TIME** 1–2 days

**DIFFICULTY** A moderate level of canoe tripping skills and experience in whitewater canoeing are needed.

**NUMBER OF PORTAGES** 17 (not all portages are necessary)

**LONGEST PORTAGE** 390 yards (358 m)

**FEE** Mississagua River is situated, for the most part, on Crown land, and no fee is needed for Canadian citizens.

**ALTERNATIVE ACCESS** Turn right, off Mississagua Dam Road and onto Mississagua/Gold Lake Road, and put in to the left of where an iron bridge crosses the river.

**ALTERNATIVE ROUTE** None

**FISH SPECIES** Bass can be caught along the entire river.

**KAYAK FRIENDLY** No

**OUTFITTERS**
WILD ROCK OUTFITTERS
169 Charlotte Street
Peterborough, Ontario
K9J 2T7
705-745-9133

ADVENTURE FITNESS
Buckhorn Road & County Road 18
R.R. 3
Lakefield, Ontario
K0L 2H0
705-652-7986

**FOR MORE INFORMATION**
MINISTRY OF NATURAL RESOURCES
Bancroft District Office
Box 500
Bancroft, Ontario
K0L 1C0
613-332-3940

**TOPOGRAPHIC MAP** 31 D/9

# Wolf Island Provincial Park

**I WAS TWELVE WHEN MY FATHER** took me on my very first canoe trip. Actually, it wasn't a true canoe trip. We were staying at a fly-in fishing lodge — something we did every summer — and spent a good part of the week trolling the main lake without much luck. By the second last day, my father and I decided to borrow one of the lodge's beat-up aluminum canoes and portage into a neighboring lake and try for speckle trout. Boy, did we catch fish.

To this day, I have always preferred the canoe over the convenience of the outboard motor. My father, however, hasn't been in one since — that is, until last year's fishing trip to Wolf Island.

The island is a relatively unknown provincial park situated along the Trent-Severn Waterway, between Lovesick Lake and Lower Buckhorn Lake. It was originally designated a Natural Environment Park for its unique geological features, where Paleozoic limestone outcroppings rub shoulders with much older Precambrian bedrock. A number of crescent-shaped gouges and striations were marked deep in the bedrock by the passing glaciers, and the mixture of swamp forest and barren rockscape make for an interesting habitat.

There's no road access directly to Wolf Island, so my father and I chose to head out from the parking lot and boat launch at the Burleigh Falls Lock, and paddle west to reach the park. The conventional lock, one of 36 found along the 422-mile (386 km) Trent-Severn Waterway and managed by Parks Canada, is located just north of the falls and on the left side of Highway 28.

It took us well over an hour to navigate through a dozen or so tiny islands, and then across an exposed stretch of Lovesick Lake before reaching Wolf Island.

It was a relaxed paddle, though. The clouds were high and the leftover mist from the night before still clung to the water's surface, making for an incredible calm. We even stopped twice along the way to pour coffee from our Thermos and make a couple of casts for walleye or a possible muskie.

Once at Wolf Island's east shore, our plan was to spend the rest of the day circling it counterclockwise. The island, as well as some of the small surrounding islands, has designated campsites. (Take note that some islands to the west are owned by Curve Lake Indian Reserve; please respect their private land). It's also a non-operating park and the campsites are free of charge. But I hadn't planned on us staying the night. Heck, it was hard enough to convince my father to sit in a canoe all day, let alone sleep on the cold ground.

To get to the opposite side of the island, there are portages around four dams (Sunrise, Sunset, Black Duck and Grey Duck), an old abandoned canoe lift-over,

*All things considered, my father took the dunking quite well.*

and the Lovesick Lock. Our choice was a 66-yard (60 m) trail around the north side of Grey Duck Dam, the second of the two dams to the north.

After a few minutes of pushing through thick weed beds and finding ourselves lost at the end of two dead-end bays, we found the proper take-out below the dam and began carrying our canoe and gear over the portage.

Things were going great so far. I managed to catch a few perch below the dam and my father managed to avoid all the poison ivy growing thick along the trail. (He's had a terrible reaction to it since using it as toilet paper years ago). Then, after successfully loading up the canoe without any mishap, everything went downhill. With my father positioned in the front seat, I pushed us off from shore, tripped on an exposed root, and tipped the canoe. In seconds, gallons of water poured in and before we could register what had happened, my father and I were both swimming in a mixture of water and swamp ooze.

All things considered, my dad took the dunking quite well. He only cursed a bit and then slowly made his way to shore, while leaving me to fish out our gear and bail out the canoe. The truth is, I thought for sure he'd call it quits right then and there. Surprisingly, though, he just poured us a third cup of coffee and then motioned us to continue on.

By noon our clothes had nearly dried out and we had caught enough perch to enjoy a shore lunch on one of the designated campsites. To get back over to Lovesick Lake, we both decided that a ride on the Lovesick Lock was a better option than portaging around another dam.

We spotted the lock station the moment we reached the south end of the island. The gatehouses along the Trent-Severn system are pretty much identical — painted brown and yellow with a perfectly manicured lawn. As we approached the lock, the huge metal gates were left open, as if the lockmaster knew of our intentions, and we paddled directly into the chamber.

# Wolf Island
# Provincial Park

28

36

BURLEIGH FALLS

**S&F**

WOLF ISLAND PROVINCIAL PARK

Black Duck Dam
P50m
Grey Duck Island
P50m
Grey Duck Dam

WOLF ISLAND PROVINCIAL PARK

abandoned canoe lift-over

Lovesick Lock

P50m

Sunset Dam
P50m
Sunrise Dam

• Alternative Access

Deer Bay Marina

North School Road

To Hwy. 28

Lovesick Lake

N

1 km

* Note: campsites on islands other than Wolf Island are a part of the Curve Lake Indian Reserve.

My dad held the canoe steady alongside the mossy concrete wall while I got out and paid the moderate fee for passage. (The charge is by the length of the vessel). I have to admit that when I returned, our boat looked a little silly floating alongside expensive yachts and assorted pleasure craft. The lockmaster waited for one more cruiser to fill the chamber and then began cranking a wheel to close the back doors. Soon we heard a gurgling noise and the water level began to drop. Lovesick Lock is the smallest in the system and we only dropped down a few feet, not much if you consider that the entire system from Balsam Lake to the Bay of Quinte drops down 600 feet (182 m). It's an enjoyable ride just the same. Eventually the doors in front of us opened up and all the boats filed out in orderly fashion. The whole process took about 10 to 15 minutes, and it would have been faster to portage. But we did manage to stay dry.

## WOLF ISLAND PROVINCIAL PARK

**DIFFICULTY** Novice

**PORTAGES** 2

**LONGEST PORTAGE** 66 yards (60 m)

**FEE** This is an unmaintained provincial park and no camping fee is required, but you have to pay for parking at the Burleigh Falls Lock or the alternative access at Deer Bay Marina.

**ALTERNATIVE ACCESS** Deer Bay Marina can be used as a way to avoid any portaging. Reach the marina by turning left off Highway 28 (just north of Young's Point) and onto North School Road. It's approximately 4.5 miles (7 km) to the marina.

**ALTERNATIVE ROUTE** Using Deer Bay Marina as an alternative access, you can simply paddle straight across to the west side of the island and make camp there.

**FISH SPECIES** The entire route provides good fishing for bass, walleye, muskellunge and perch.

**KAYAK FRIENDLY** Yes

**OUTFITTERS**
WILD ROCK OUTFITTERS
169 Charlotte Street
Peterborough, Ontario K9J 2T7
705-745-9133

ADVENTURE FITNESS
Buckhorn Road & County Road 8
R.R. 3
Lakefield, Ontario
K0L 2H0
705-652-7986

**FOR MORE INFORMATION**
TRENT-SEVERN WATERWAY
Box 567
Peterborough, Ontario K9J 6Z6
705-742-9267

**TOPOGRAPHICAL MAP**
Burleigh Falls 31 D/9

# A Note on Environmental Ethics

**CANOEING IN COTTAGE COUNTRY** is a double-edged sword. On one side you have a series of quick and easy trips that are extremely accessible. They are hassle free for the most part, especially the routes that are not a part of a managed park. Basically, they are perfect for urban dwellers wanting to escape for a weekend in the wilderness. On the other side, however, you have the major problem of overuse. Campsites are littered with garbage and toilet paper mounds. Portages aren't properly maintained and are being abused by other recreationists, such as ATV operators. And the main reason why people first used the area, to get way from it all, quickly disappears.

So how do we keep the routes as pristine as they once were? Well, we can't. Some believe that these semi-wild places should be kept a secret. Not only is that impossible in such a developed area, it's also selfish. Others have fought against the lack of government management over the routes and organized volunteer groups to maintain and watch over them. This is a fantastic idea but in no way the absolute answer. Each group member will always have his or her own separate agendas, creating tension in the groups, and many volunteers will find themselves becoming burnt out. That's why the government should be held responsible, which doesn't look likely at this point in time. The only possible solution in the long term is to create some type of environmental ethic among the users themselves. Here are a few suggestions:

## CHOOSING A CAMPSITE

The majority of canoe routes in cottage country have been developed on Crown land or undeveloped provincial parks, which means campsites found along the way are not designated. There's no law stating you must stay at a particular spot. However, to lessen your impact on the area you should always make use of the heavier impacted sites rather than "improve" on a new site.

Small island sites should be avoided at all costs. They can never withstand the abuse and are guaranteed to become a magnet for nuisance bears in the area.

Never dig trenches around your tent or cut down standing trees. Tents should be placed on bare rock devoid of any plant life if possible. And if not, then choose fauna such as meadow grass that can withstand being slept on much better than blueberry bushes. And when you are leaving your site, make sure you depart with everything you came with. Nothing should be left behind.

*The best way to protect these accessible canoe routes is to create some sort of environmental ethic among the users themselves.*

## GROUP SIZE

Regulated parks, such as Algonquin or Killarney, have a limit of group sizes allowed in the interior. Only nine canoeists are permitted to camp on each designated site. The number seems odd, since canoeists usually travel in pairs. Traditionally, however, local camps would have three children per canoe, and it was the camps that made most of the heavy impact on the park's campsites. The same problem is now happening on cottage country routes. As the majority of these routes exist on Crown land or non-regulated parks, group sizes are not limited. That means large organized groups will choose to paddle these areas rather than operating provincial parks. It's not that they are actually being malicious. In fact, most of them are far more environmentally conscious than other users.

They have even gone out of their way in the past few years to clean up the canoe routes that are no longer being maintained by the government. However, the problem still remains. If you have too many people making use of a campsite, it will definitely be detrimental to the natural surroundings. Therefore, large groups should split up to make camp, having one leader per seven kids.

## WASHING UP

The days of washing dishes at the water's edge are gone. Even if you are using biodegradable soap, the bacteria from greasy pots and pans create a major problem. It's also a very ineffective way to do dishes. It's far better to fill a pot with warm water, walk back from the shoreline at least 33 yards (30 m), and, using pine needles and sand as a scrub brush, wash up and then deposit the gray water in a small cat hole.

Washing yourself away from shoreline is even more important. So many canoeists become ill from getting their drinking water in the same area where others have cleaned up, especially after they've just relieved themselves. Again, fill a pot with water and walk back at least 33 yards (30 m) in the backwoods.

## CAT HOLES AND TREASURE CHESTS

Toilet paper mounds have to be one of the worst things to find littering a campsite. It can ruin the entire trip. If there isn't a treasure chest (makeshift out-house) made available on the site, go back at least 55 yards (50 m) from camp, turn up at least 2 inches (3-4 cm) of topsoil and, when finished, cover up the waste and toilet paper with a mound of dirt, just as a cat does in a litter box. In two weeks or less the waste matter will become perfect potting soil.

Feminine hygiene products should be either burned in a hot fire or carried out in a plastic bag. Do not dispose of them by burying them. Wild animals, especially squirrels and bears, will be attracted to the strong scent of the pheromones and dig them up, decorating the camp with them.

## FIRES VS. STOVES

Campfires are an important part of the camping experience. However, with so many places now becoming void of dead wood, sites are being stripped of living trees as well as essential cover for fauna and flora. So, as a rule, campfires should be thought of as a luxury, not a necessity. A stove is much faster for cooking meals than a fire, and creates less of an impact on a site. When choosing a stove to purchase, make sure that it runs on white gas rather than butane or propane. This takes away any chance of someone leaving an empty gas cylinder behind, which is becoming a major problem in the interior.

# Bibliography

Barry, James P. *Georgian Bay: The Sixth Great Lake*. Toronto: Clarke, Irwin and Company Limited, 1968.

Blackstone Harbour (Massasauga Wildlands) Provincial Park: Interim Management Statement. Ontario Ministry of Natural Resources.

Brown, Ron. *50 Unusual Things to See in Ontario*. Erin, Ontario: The Boston Mills Press, 1989.

*Burnt River System Canoe Routes* map. Ontario Ministry of Natural Resources, Minden District.

*Canoe Muskoka-Haliburton* map. Ontario Ministry of Natural Resources, Bracebridge District.

*Canoe Routes of Ontario*. Parks and Recreational Areas Branch of the Ontario Ministry of Natural Resources in cooperation with McClelland and Stewart, 1981.

Cole, A.O.C. and Jean Murray Cole, eds. *Kawartha Heritage: Proceedings of the Kawartha Conference*. Peterborough Historical Atlas Foundation, 1981.

Cole, Jean Murray. *The Loon Calls: A History of the Township of Chandos*. Municipality of the Township of Chandos, 1989.

Craig, John and Nickels, Nick. *The Lunge Hunter: The Life and Times of Alex Sharpe*. Privately published, 1983.

Cummings, H.R. *Early Days in Haliburton*. Toronto: Ontario Department of Lands and Forests (Ontario Ministry of Natural Resources), 1963.

Drew, Wayland, and Bruce Littlejohn. *Superior: The Haunted Shore*. Toronto: Gage, 1975.

*Echoes of the Past: Resounding in the Present*. Ontario Ministry of Natural Resources.

Fox, William Sherwood. *The Bruce Beckons*. Toronto: University of Toronto Press, 1952.

Frost, Leslie M. *Forgotten Pathways of the Trent*. Don Mills, Ontario: Burns and MacEachern, 1973.

*Gibson River Canoe Route* map. Ontario Ministry of Natural Resources, Parry Sound District.

Grigg, Muriel Rogers. *Magnetic Muskoka*. Baxter Press, 1971.

Hodgins, Bruce W. *Nastawagan: The Canadian North by Canoe and Snowshoe*. Toronto: Betelgeuse Books, 1985.

Huffman, Doris. *Kawartha Park by Path and Paddle*. Archival Committee of Smith Township, 1987.

James, Mac. "The Great Outdoors." *Haliburton Highlands Destinations Guide*. Central Ontario Travel Association Haliburton Highlands Chamber of Commerce, 1990.

*Land Tenure: Bancroft District*. Ontario Ministry of Natural Resources, Bancroft District, Algonquin Region, 1988.

*Leslie M. Frost Natural Resource Centre* map. Ontario Ministry of Natural Resources, Surveys, Mapping and Remote Sensing Branch, Minden and Bracebridge Districts, 1988.

Long, Gary. *This River The Muskoka*. Erin, Ontario: The Boston Mills Press, 1989.

Mallory, Enid. *Kawartha: Living on These Lakes*. Peterborough Publishing, 1991.

*Minden District Fishing Map & Guide*. Ontario Ministry of Natural Resources, Minden District.

Morse, Eric W. *Freshwater Saga: Memoirs of a Lifetime of Wilderness Canoeing in Canada*. Toronto: University of Toronto Press, 1987.

*North Kawartha Canoe Routes* map. Ontario Ministry of Natural Resources, Minden and Bancroft Districts.

Pryke, Susan. *Exploring Muskoka*. Erin, Ontario: The Boston Mills Press, 1987.

"The Publications of the Champlain Society, Ontario Series VI, Muskoka and Haliburton 1615-1875." Toronto Champlain Society, 1963.

Reid, Ron and Janet Grand. *Canoeing Ontario's Rivers*. Vancouver, Toronto: Douglas and McIntyre, 1985.

Reynolds, Nila. *In Quest of Yesterday*. Provisional County of Haliburton, Minden, Ontario, 1968.

Scott, Guy. *History of Kinmount: A Community on the Fringe*. Kinmount, Ontario: John Deyell Co., 1987.

*South Georgian Bay Canoe Routes* map. Ontario Ministry of Natural Resources, Parry Sound District.

Terpstra, Ron. *Historical Report: Blackstone Harbour (Massasauga Wildlands) Provincial Park*. Ontario Ministry of Natural Resources, Parry Sound District, 1991.

Thomas, W.D. *Bobcaygeon: The Hub of the Kawarthas: A History of the Village and Its Surroundings*. Privately published, 1980.

Vastokas, Joan M. and Roman K. Vastokas. *Sacred Art of the Algonkians: A Study of the Peterborough Petroglyphs*. Peterborough, Ontario: Mansard Press, 1973.

Vickery, Jim Dale. "Going Alone." Canoe Magazine, June 1985.

*The Warbler: A Newsletter About Planning Blackstone Harbour (Massasauga Wildlands) Provincial Park*. Ontario Ministry of Natural Resources, 1991.

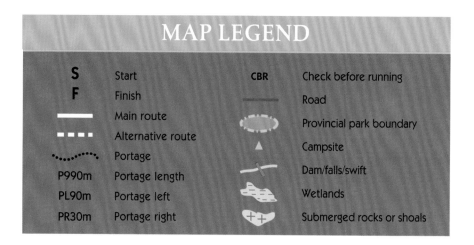

## MAP LEGEND

| | | | |
|---|---|---|---|
| **S** | Start | **CBR** | Check before running |
| **F** | Finish | | Road |
| | Main route | | Provincial park boundary |
| | Alternative route | | Campsite |
| | Portage | | Dam/falls/swift |
| P990m | Portage length | | |
| PL90m | Portage left | | Wetlands |
| PR30m | Portage right | | Submerged rocks or shoals |